A Himalayan Pilgrim

A Himalayan Pilgrim

A TREK TO EVEREST

or 'A Himalayan Pilgrim'

Written by James Joyce
Kathmandu, Nepal

A HIMALAYAN PILGRIM

Table of Contents

Maps

Nepal

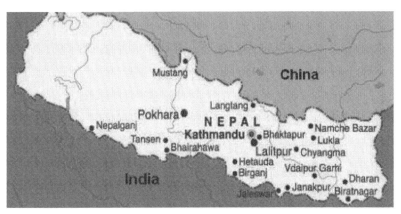

Everest Base Camp Area

Changes

I finally did it and booked the flights. Clicking 'pay now' felt like the beginning of the adventure even though I was still a month away from leaving and had a family holiday and trip to Mexico with Glaiza to look forward to.

In truth, Everest, Nepal, Tibet and India had been on my bucket list from a very early point, after China they had always been next. But as with all things, life gets in the way and in my case that had certainly been the case.

This trip had been scheduled for the tail end of 2014 as part of a grand adventure to end my sojourn in China and move back to the UK with my then partner. This plan was to fall apart spectacularly, so after having flights booked, itineraries planned and equipment's prepared (literally packed) I abandoned this to be home with my family. At the time I was in no state to undertake such an ambitious, challenging, life changing and spiritual experience, I could think of nothing better at that moment than being with my loved ones to help me through a difficult period of readjustment; Which they did.

As the months passed by, I relocated from my hometown to London, the big smoke, to begin a career in finance - a sensible job. I had the girl of my dreams in my best friend from College living nearby, a house share in Brentford near the glamour of Chiswick and greenery of Richmond and a stable job in a funky, modern office. What more could I wish for?

And yet this was not to last.

My mother was re diagnosed with cancer of the neck and throat just as life was beginning to settle down and I was getting into the swing of things. I remember the phone call I received from my brother vividly when after a check-up he called me to tell me "it's back Jimmy." My heart sank, I could have vomited. Looking out from the glass cubicle I could see my colleagues going about their business as usual, outside I could see delivery drivers pulling up to the building and cyclists heading to the lake, and yet in this small room my world had literally stopped. My brothers next line confirmed what I already knew, "there is nothing they can do."

Within 6 weeks my girlfriend and I had moved back, I quit my job to take care of my mother. One of the deepest regrets of my life up to that point was not taking time out when my father was also diagnosed with cancer. He subsequently passed away and every day since I wish I had been with him in his final days, to just be there and savour his presence. At the time he had said he didn't want anyone, and so the responsibility of taking care of him had fallen onto my devoted and loving mother. In all honesty at the time I couldn't dream of quitting a job, fears about money and the risk of not getting another meant I took the sensible choices rather than the ones I wanted to. If only I could go back in time and make myself change my mind, if only.

This time with my mother it felt like an opportunity to not make the same mistake again. She, my brother and I thought, was not strong (how wrong we were!) and so I wanted to be with her and make sure that in the time she had left she would never be or feel alone. I wanted to make sure that she could end her days with as much dignity as she deserved and to be able to do it the way she wanted – at home. I aslo needed to be there for my brother. When I had left for China years earlier it had been as a rebound to the loss of our father, I had struggled at his passing terribly. My brother however had been the man of the house and had stayed, probably not his choice, but in spite of this he had taken on the role and responsibility of both parent and home. He had been chivalrous and unselfish and in a small way I hoped that my gesture, to help our mother was also helping him. I was and am eternally grateful for the role he played after our fathers passing. He showed himself to be a far stronger and better man than me.

The status quo didn't last long and before we knew it, we were stood in the kitchen the morning after the funeral. I was jobless and now without purpose. I had spent so much of my energies and focus on one thing, I now felt redundant. Before long reality struck, I needed to plug back into the system.

Being unemployed is all well and good and sure having holidays and breaks is something everyone dreams of. The reality is somewhat different after the novelty wears off within a couple of weeks. Endless, mindless daytime TV, dwindling financial capability and boredom conspire to make even the strongest will wilt, so that feeling blue and long lethargic lie-ins become the norm. Stagnation.

"You need to go away," Glaiza would say; I was not really convinced, although privately it was what I wanted a large part of me thought I should just get back to work, back to routine and back to people. I was struggling again without my mother and without the purpose she had provided. I had been to Church more times in the daytime than ever before and had made numerous visits to the graves just for a chat. I missed both parents terribly.

Although I am a practicing Catholic, I have always had a keen interest in all things spiritual. During this period I read voraciously on Hindusim and Buddhism, anything that could help answer the big questions, anything that could give my soul some kind of peace as no matter how many times I prayed, I still felt empty. Upon my mother's passing I felt a void inside, a hole. Glaiza knew I needed something to help me move forward. Returning to work immediately was unthinkable, for want of a better phrase I needed to rebalance my qi, I needed to feed my soul and find myself again, to rebuild and move forward. I saw this trip, this ever present on my bucket list, Nepal and Everest as the obvious choice and indeed the best opportunity to meditate on events and have the spiritual rebalancing and reawakening I was looking for. Walking alone in the Himalaya with the Goddess of the mountains, Chomolungma.

I was going to Nepal.

Weston-super-Mare, England
Sunday 17th January 2016 23:21pm

Mum and Dad, who are my inspirations,

Willy, who is always there for me,

Glaiza, my rock,

And the boys, it's your turn next.

Preparation

Once the decision was made, I then had to go and sort the actuals of the trip. It was quite an overwhelming moment sat in front of a screen with a destination but no real concept of how it was going to come together. There were so many things to think about, from the clothing to general equipment – what would I need? Would I need a stove and camping gear? I was heading into the highest mountain range in the world, albeit at the end of February, would it be in the high minuses meaning thick thermals or would this only be on the last couple of days as I reached higher elevations? What would Kathmandu be like?

Being a bit of a bookworm, I relished the chance to get stuck into the travel tips, maps and histories. Reports of hiking trails, climbing stories and the day-to-day goings on of where I was heading, I needed to know it all.

I then had to work out the actual logistics of the trip. It was not a forgone conclusion with Glaiza how long I could go for and I didn't want to push it. I had sketched an outline for a month away though did consider longer depending on her views, particularly I had the idea to visit a monastery but knew that this would definitely be in the realms of 'taking the mickey' and not likely to be green lit, as nice an idea as it was. Also, I had no intention or desire to be away from Glaiza for such an extended period, as much as I was eager to get to the mountains. Without being too soppy, you know you have found your partner for life when you no longer make these decisions in isolation and the thought of being away from them or out of contact for more than a couple of days in this technological age is really quite unfathomable.

Lastly there was the physical preparation to consider. This was probably the aspect I was least prepared for or at least had minimal understanding, that was until I had done some reading around the dangers of altitude sickness and generally the physical requirements of heading into the Himalayan range, especially as I was intending to do it alone not being part of a tour group, which was strictly not advised.

All my plans were slowly coalescing, my reading list was growing, my trip was all but settled in terms of plan and I had started to exercise to lose a few extra pounds, I am never the leanest guy at the best of times yo-yoing throughout the year. I knew if I was going to stand any chance of achieving this dream of base camp, let alone enjoy it, I had to be a bit fitter.

And so, with this final aspect in mind, as it was really the last thing to think about, I proposed a little break for Glaiza and I. She had a bit of time off so I thought I would like to treat her to a few days away in the great outdoors – kill two birds with one stone as it were. So, what better way to show her how much I appreciated her than a few days away in some spa or other in the lovely rolling scenery of the Lake District (followed by an assault on Englands highest peak - Scafell Pike.) To be fair Glaiza was on board for a little trek having been with me to Snowdonia on her 30th birthday, another one of my little 'surprises', and it was an excellent opportunity to try out some of my new gear.

The first day involved a scenic drive and very relaxing evening filled with a delicious dinner and bubble bath. The relaxation was short lived however as day two was the trek. We got up early and enjoyed a pair of grand gut-busting breakfasts anticipating the exertion to come. After a false start where I set us off via an extended route that was almost impassable due to heavy rains, we returned to the car to make our way to the foot of the trail proper.

The initial walk had itself proved eye opening, as it was extremely muddy with lake like puddles and soft ground everywhere. By itself this wasn't an issue, but it did make the going slow. The clue was here very early on as to the state of the path up to the peak, had we drawn the connections we might have considered the bloated streams, as it was we walked for a good hour up a steep stairway, sloshing through mud puddles and hopping over the small streams that were working their way down the mountainside.

The route zigzagged upwards following the expanding and deepening stream. Very quickly it was clear that one would not be able to walk through but would have to wade through the water, it had built up its size very quickly. Glaiza was not happy about this prospect, as the path at places cut straight across the water, which in drier times was not an issue, with melting snows and heavy rainfall the 'stream' was a veritable river. We shot off the main path up a bank on the left seeing if we could join farther up, this was not what she had signed up for, an off piste off route hike up a mountain wading through rivers and swimming through mud. Before long she sat down on a step looking rather forlorn. I knew exactly what she was thinking. It was over.

The week after I couldn't let it lie. Glaiza was away, so at 11:05 on a Monday night I booked a hotel again by Lake Windemere and made the choice to head up again to Scafell Pike to try again the next morning, I would not be defeated.

This mentality is something I have always had, a bit impulsive, some might say reckless. I am however very good at following through, once my mind is on something I am like a dog with the proverbial bone.

In the week that had passed since our aborted venture the snows had continued to melt to the point that the run off had ran off so that the streams that had crisscrossed the walking trail from the south side of the mountain were now traversable and no longer impassable.

Both trips had been useful for different reasons. Understanding how I felt with a bag was a big step, although I would never be able to prepare for the altitude, I felt confident in my ability to trek with a 15kg pack. It was apparent to me as I drove home feeling pleased with the decision to try again I knew that that no matter what I did, the reality would be something else no doubt, however physically I was as ready as I could be, logistically I was all set, and mentally I was already there.

Day 2- Kathmandu

28/2/2016

I'm sat at the end of my first day, 5pm, in the Garden of Dreams. A leftover relic of some old 'colonial' gardens complex replete with ponds and fountains, bushes, multicoloured flowers and creepers climbing their way up steel trellises. Amazingly this piece of paradise is but a stone's throw away from the madness that is Thamel, the tourist hub of Kathmandu.

After wandering the smoggy dusty city what better way than to relax in the genuinely pretty gardens with a plethora of Nepalese couples stealing themselves away from the busy city for some apparent down time and a kiss and cuddle.

There was a very quaint coffee shop in the corner of the gardens with waist coated waiters and beers so extortionate as to be eye widening. I settled for an Americano. Sitting, soaking up the atmosphere and waiting for my drink I thought I would start my Himalaya journal.

Day 1 – Home

27/2/2016

With my bag packed and it feeling a little bit heavier than I intended it to be, I set off. First stop was Glaiza and then a drive to Heathrow. After an emotional goodbye she would be heading on to Gatwick and work, as she was cabin crew. At least she would have something to focus for the first few hours after our goodbye, she had already been making comments about how she was going to miss me in the weeks leading up to the trip, I was pretty sure the farewell would be difficult.

Dumping my bag and rucksack on the back seat not for the first time I was wondering if I was overreaching myself trying to do the Everest Base Camp trek alone, without a guide or a porter. Time would tell.

We had a pleasant drive, although Glaiza was clearly upset and a bit withdrawn. I tried to keep her positive and her spirits up. After checking in my rucksack, we shared an emotional farewell, I too had a little lump in my throat. Knowing I wasn't going to see her for an extended period and knowing that we would have limited contact was not nice to contemplate. However, the thought of a few weeks alone, in the mountains, with nothing but the heavens and my thoughts was something I truly needed, it was a sacrifice in this moment I was willing to make.

We both looked at each other across the barrier and waved, eventually we both turned and went our own ways; it was the beginning of the adventure. As I went through to departures I was overcome with adrenaline, excitement and nerves – I hadn't done something like this on my own since a trip to Cambodia in 2012, a lot had happened since then and this trip was going to be an opportunity to hopefully end what had been a turbulent chapter in my life.

The journey itself would take me via Doha (Qatar) before arriving at 7pm on the 27th February. I slept on the second flight next to a Nepali guy who seemed very uncomfortable next to me. I smiled, said hello ('Namaste') and had given him space when he had tried to move. Still there was no smile, not even an acknowledgement of any sort. Never mind, I thought, I would just sleep through.

Thankfully I had prepared ahead of time and had arranged my visa online which meant after getting off the plane I wasn't scrambling between desks for bits of paper. I simply had to pay and then collect my stamp as I passed through after telling the customs officer about the plans for my time in Nepal, I am sure every foreigner has a similar story with huge back packs, new trekking equipment and that wide eyed look of someone clearly jet lagged but bursting with excitement to be there. With 30 days in my passport, more than enough, I was heading towards the luggage reclaim.

Tribhuvan International Airport, the main airport in Nepal was tiny, which really struck me especially seeing as this was a capital airport. This was the first time I had actually, really contemplated the reality that Nepal was a small, relatively poor nation that had been through traumatic event after traumatic event in recent decades. I had of course done my reading but seeing things firsthand can often appear starker than simple words on a page. My first impression was certainly not of wealth, nor even of a country prepared for mass tourism, which if the tourist board could get itself together could be an incredible source of income for the country with the vast areas of natural beauty for outdoors people and the opportunity for spiritual enlightenment for others being an extremely religiously diverse nation (Hindu and Buddhist primarily). Later, many people I met would talk of corruption as a major snag in the country's development, which explains a lot. The scruffy appearance and dated décor of the airport as well as the lack of locals (mainly foreigners) milling about did not suggest a thriving economy. Then again, maybe I was being quick to judge, I had just landed and was soaking up the initial ambience. As a trekker (who was also looking to for something spiritual) I had come at the end of the off-season just before the high season where the temperatures in the mountains begin to rapidly increase along with the number of people. I would see this on the way back from my trek and indeed that Kathmandu and more specifically Thamel was a thriving hub.

My bag seemed to take an eternity to arrive on the belt. There were a number of groups also waiting for theirs, local guides were pulling off huge identical blue packs, red packs, and black packs all carrying the logos of a specific tour group. I had considered doing this trip as part of a group, but after researching and really contemplating my motivations for heading to Nepal I realized that a) I wanted to be alone, and b) it was possible to do it alone relatively safely and cheaply, if you stuck to the known routes and didn't push yourself outside of your known limits.

I was still waiting for my bag.

My bag was a 60-litre rucksack, packed to just around 20kg. I knew this would be difficult, especially trekking at altitude. I had planned for 15-17kg maximum, but as so often happens one packs last minute items that you definitely cannot survive without, that ironically never get taken from the bag. However, I thought if I took my time, I should be okay, just about.

After waiting half an hour I went to the bathroom and started to question what I would do if my bag didn't arrive, I always worry when I have a connecting flight and having traveled many times on connecting flights and suffered the hassle of delayed bags, I was beginning to get a little 'squeezy'. There was nothing of great value in my bag, but the collective spend especially on clothing was not small, and more importantly the gear was specific to the needs of the trip. A lot of the gear for trekking can get quite expensive and I had spent a few hundred pounds upgrading a lot of my more worn out clothing and equipment.

Just as I was getting seriously concerned (and stood almost on my own) my bag appeared on the belt. 'Hurrah' I thought and immediately made my way to the exit to find a ride to the Mountain Peace Guest House, instantly forgetting the anxiety of moments before.

Earlier in the week I had emailed the guesthouse as they had said they offer airport pickup. Scanning the area outside the main door I couldn't see anyone with my name. Fortunately, the lack of response to my two emails had prepared me for this so I just found a taxi. 7 dollars quoted which didn't sound too ridiculous but then again what did I know? If I was at home in the UK 7 dollars would be more than fine for the type of distance we were looking at. Experience taught me though that taxi drivers take advantage of new arrivals and so I was wary. He seemed a cheerful chap so what the hell, throwing my pack in the back of his Suzuki Maruti I jumped in the front.

The roads were interesting, craters and potholes everywhere and no road markings. I can safely say that the mooted suggestion of the British Government that no road markings could lead to slower and safer driving is definitely not the case!

I sat in the back seat as we weaved our way through the traffic and around the various obstacles the road offered. Another guy had jumped in the car who seemed to know the driver and also spoke English, this hadn't alarmed me initially, maybe I should have been more cautious but it really didn't occur to me and I used the opportunity to pump the man for information, which initially he gladly offered. Eventually though he produced a business card, and surprise surprise he owned a tour company – of course he did. He wanted me to agree to a tour with him as early on in our chat I had mentioned my intention to go to base camp alone. He had said that in no uncertain terms was I to do this, it wasn't safe to do alone and very dangerous, so I would of course, need him. Plus, he was extremely reasonable he said, in comparison to others. As politely as I could I declined his offer but said if I were to change my mind, he would be my first choice of guide. Exiting the car and taking my bag from the back seat the man seemed very frustrated, and a little desperate following me more than a few steps from the car after I had paid and waved farewell. Clearly this was a typical way he picked up business. Sadly for him, I was determined and not very malleable. Walking away from his loud exhalations and tutting I was sure this would not be the last time I would be having this type of conversation.

Making my way up a (very) dimly lit alley I struggled to see where I was going. There were no streetlights and the path was a hotchpotch of stones and sand. In the twilight it was extremely dangerous if you were not careful, each treacherous step a lottery as to where your foot could fall. In the shadows I noticed on a sign the grainy low definition print of the word guesthouse. Assuming this might be mine I made my way towards it, tip toeing up the alleyway. As I entered the dingy reception area two teenage boys looked up from behind a counter (or at least I thought they were teenage initially, but after talking to them I think they might have been in their early twenties.) Neither spoke very good English but we managed to establish that they didn't have any reservation for me, probably why no one had come to meet me from the airport. No problem though, I was quite relaxed and rightly so as they both beamed and exclaimed "great room" followed by "the best!" I smiled hopefully.

After following the enthusiastic pair up three flights of stairs they unlocked a door to a space to which I can only describe as functional. Yes, there was a bed, and a chair, and a bedside table, the decoration was grey (or faded/dirty white) and the place looked like it could do with more than a lick of paint. However, after travelling for so long, and being quite exhausted it was more than enough, in fact the bed was positively calling out to me. I hadn't paid for luxury and hadn't wished it. This trip was not about that.

Looking in the shower room the shower was much like those in China, sat directly above the sink and right next to the toilet, economizing with space but perfect for multi-tasking. The bed proved to be extremely firm; what was supposedly a mattress had seen better days but at least the yellowing sheets smelt fresh. One of the boys (distinguishable from the other by a spiky mullet and a thin fluffy moustache) was smiling maniacally flicking a light switch on and off. I twigged instantly – electricity. A solitary lightbulb gave off a dim light, enough to potter about at least. As far as I understood this light was working off a generator so that even when the city was in a 'load shedding' phase this light would work.

Load Shedding is where the government imposes fixed power outages across the city to cope with the insatiable demand for power. The time where they suffer the most is in winter and before spring when the water level is at its lowest and thus the hydroelectric system which accounts for a large portion of the nation's power can't produce enough wattage for the growing number of phone chargers and appliances. Each day the load shedding is spread across Kathmandu's districts for periods of up to 13 hours at a time. I wondered if running water would be affected too?

My young friends lingered awkwardly for a moment or so expecting a tip probably. I didn't think so, especially after my reservation had disappeared. I smiled and began unpacking. Visibly disappointed they left, 'sorry mate' I thought as for the second time I heard loud exhalations and tuts from a local.

Unboxing the new universal adapter that Glaiza had bought me I charged my near dead iPad, iPod and iPhone, (I am currently typing this on a Mac...I may not have come for luxury but even in this day and age there were items I could not live without.) I was trying to make the most of the limited electricity before it went off not fully knowing the schedule. Feeling a little peckish I decided to go for a little wander around the block and get something to eat.

It was still quite dark, not just down the alley but seemingly everywhere. I wasn't to know at the time but within moments of me plugging in my items for charging the power went off for load shedding and so all of the lights along the street and in the buildings mostly went off (unless they were making use of petrol/diesel generators) causing me to walk like an old man watching where my feet landed as I went, I would get better and more confident, I would have to considering where I was intending to go. As I made my way up the street in no direction in particular there were innumerable stray dogs pottering about unafraid of man or machine, taking very little notice of me as I passed. More than once I almost turned an ankle, I put this down to tiredness more than anything, so I thought I'd find somewhere to stop off at the earliest opportunity.

Literally on the next corner there was a sign saying, 'Hole in the Wall', they did food, beer and coffee. Perfect.

The steps up to the first floor were no more than a ladder, not the easiest in my hiking boots, the only alternative in my bag were flip-flops. I wasn't to know at this point, but these boots were going to be the best footwear I have ever had, I was going to be literally living in them over the next few weeks.

Climbing off the ladder onto the first floor there was westerner sat wearing a bandana surrounded by beer bottles. The walls were adorned with lots of western paraphernalia like movie posters and flags.

"Hey" I said, "you have any beer?" I knew this was a bit of a redundant question as I could see the fridge and a vast number of empty bottles displayed in front of him.

"Sure" he answered, I couldn't tell an accent. He proceeded to go to the fridge and pulled out a Tiger beer – 7% volume, stronger than back home. I sat down opposite; there were two small tables with equally small benches with little cushions to soften the feel on the bottom. As I sat sipping my beer a Nepali guy came down the ladder from the floor above and burst into giggles along with my western friend opposite. They exchanged a few words and I established that the westerner was called Vale (Banjo to his friends) and was in fact Finnish. He was also a customer. The owner didn't mind in the least that I had essentially helped myself to his produce as both he and Banjo were giggling like children. It was evident from their demeanour and moist bloodshot eyes that they were both high! I was going to see this throughout my time in Nepal that it, and more importantly Thamel in Kathmandu was a bit of a hippie haven. This made for an extremely interesting, colourful time.

I politely declined the proffered joint though greatly appreciated the beer and sandwich he made for me. Chatting with the owner was entertaining, and I was surprised to hear that he had just moved home from Woolwich where he had been resident. Sadly, he was an Arsenal fan, I wasn't going to hold it against him. He had left Nepal during the civil war which had been fought between the Maoist insurgents of the Communist Party of Nepal (CPN-M) and the government over a decade, from 1996 to 2006 culminating in the end of 240 years of continuous rule and the overthrow of the monarchy leading to the establishment of a People's Republic. Reportedly there were almost 20,000 deaths with the displacement, both internally and externally of many more, like the owner of this small bar. He only just felt it was safe enough and financially viable to return home for him to start his business. From the grin on his face he was clearly in a good place.

A Canadian named Tony then came in; he had just come back from the Everest Base Camp trek and was more than happy to share some advice, although he too was quite high so kept straying off topic. That day he had been skateboarding around Thamel, as you do, with a 'GoPro' camera weaving in and out of the bustling traffic. He seemed to enjoy the danger. His opinion was that Base Camp was definitely doable alone, however I was cautious to take too much of what he said on board as he showed videos of his antics over the day, he was clearly a risk taker, and definitely mad!

All three wanted to go and see some live music but I was tired so took the opportunity to 'nip' off once they went upstairs for another smoke beforehand. Before you wonder, I had already paid my bill. Both westerners had been in Nepal for 2 months, both had spent most of that time in either Kathmandu or (Annapurna) getting drunk and high, a very enlightening and spiritual journey no doubt, but one I was not interested in the slightest.

Day 2 – Kathmandu

28/2/2016

I hadn't showered the night before when I had arrived despite apparent hot water, I had been too lazy and too tired. How much did I regret this decision the next morning when I woke at 5am to the busy sounds of hectic roads and construction. Apparently, Kathmandu was an early riser. At about 7am I gave up trying to get back to sleep and went to shower, what a mistake that was as nothing but cold water flowed. I tried to put on a light as despite the risen sun my window looked out onto the alley and a close wall meaning it was hard to see. No light came on as there was no electricity.

Dressing I went down to get some breakfast as I had been told the night before it was from 7am, this was a clue as to the wake time, I guess.

As I sat in the 'cosy' dining area it was the owner, an Indian making his fortune in Nepal that served me a delicious omelette, orange juice and tar like coffee – absolutely fabulous! He seemed disappointed when he asked if I had enjoyed the hot water that morning, he said there was a tank that stored it to allow for the outages, however the sheer volume of guests and the fact the city woke early must have meant I was not the first to jump into the shower. I emphasised I didn't mind and that I was more than satisfied with my room, it was more than adequate for what I needed it for. At this he smiled and seemed at ease. Then we began talking about what there was to do and trips whilst I was there. Believe it or not he said he could arrange something for me at a good price, not the first time I had heard that, and I had been in the country less than 24 hours.

I looked at his travel board and my eyes were immediately drawn to a picture of a monastery clinging to a cliff edge, like something out of an old Chinese painting, incredible. The owner saw my interest and came over to tell me about Bhutan. I had always been fascinated by the Himalayan kingdom and remember watching Michael Palin visit and being mesmerised by his experiences. I wondered if me going was feasible, I wasn't sure of the logistics or cost – he would get back to me. I had a month to spend in Nepal and had various ideas for trips once I had hopefully achieved base camp. Although I wasn't sure how long this in itself was going to take, whether I would have sufficient time to visit Bhutan wasn't clear. Lumbini, the birthplace of the Buddha was high on my list, so too were the jungles of Chitwan as well as the beautiful lake town of Pokhara that serves as the entrance and exit of the grand Annapurna trek. So much to see and so little time.

I got out my map of the city as I was intending to go and get my paperwork for the trek, I needed something called a TIMS. The owner asked what I wanted and after a quick chat asked if I could wait while he made a phone call before I could leave. Later, the relevance of the call became apparent.

The sun was slowly rising along with the temperature, as I stepped out of the alleyway I was swept along by the passing traffic and was spellbound by what I saw, it was incredible – what a vision by day.

My initial thoughts of a crumbling city, almost decrepit was not far wrong, but what you could not feel at night was the character, the vibe and the energy; the sense of life going about its business was intoxicating.

Meandering down the streets and alleys of Thamel with the steady stream of human, animal and mechanical traffic I found myself in the old city with stupas and shrines dotted all about, they were magnificent. Some literally centred in the middle of main roads, and not like some old relic long forgotten and ignored by the populace, they were still 'used'. An actual part of everyday life still adorned with flowers, candles and incense. They were even used to hang washing lines, for resting bowls as people washed and centres of the congregating community, it was not important that it may have sat in the middle of a road. It was fascinating.

Clicking away with my camera I was stopped numerous times by 'students' wanting to 'practice English.' Now having travelled a fair bit I am more than aware that this often means come have a look at my shop, so after the conversation drifted on to their artworks and art schools I politely declined having to eventually just say I wanted to walk alone. I felt so rude, but it was necessary, I just wanted to soak up the atmosphere as I made my way to the ticket office. Day one and I had already shut down the hawkers – mental note to self – 'must be friendly' I thought.

I wandered towards the tourist office along roads and through alleys, parade grounds and bus stations asking lots of directions as I went, there were no discernible road signs and the layout was so haphazard one lost all sense of location. Eventually however I was stood outside a grand clean red building. Entering via a large gated entrance I spied a security guard sat behind a huge mahogany desk. He looked, stood and then called over to me, 'James?' he said, I was stunned. 'TIMS is through there'. The guesthouse owner had obviously called ahead.

Passing down the corridor I entered a much smaller room covered in posters and maps of the scenic areas of Nepal. I was a bit early for the office workers, although it was 10:30am it was a national day and so it seemed not everyone was working. To be honest throughout my time in Nepal I realized that time keeping was certainly a very vague concept. As I completed my form, a middle-aged pony tailed American came in and sat across from me, we had a brief chat. He was intending to do the earthquake hit Langtang trek, this one was meant to be only for groups because of the dangers after the earthquake though he seemed quite assured that he knew what he was doing and could do it alone. He was not what I would call a friendly man, that became acutely evident when a little later a pair of Dutch guys asked to borrow his pen, he just said 'No'. So cold! I gave them mine gladly and we shared a smile between us.

Ten minutes later and 400 rupees lighter I had my permit and my Sagarmartha National Park ticket. It was all so real now. A little tired even though it was just gone 11 I decided to head back to my guesthouse, grab a coffee and then maybe a power nap. Already I was finding the coffee in Nepal surprisingly good, strong and not too smokey.

My power nap was in danger of becoming the whole afternoon, so with much difficulty I forced myself to get up. I had skipped lunch so thought I might grab something out, I decided to head to the famous Swayambhunath Stupa, or Monkey Temple as it is commonly known, about an hour's leisurely walk west of the city.

Strolling through the suburbs I was struck by the amount of rubbish, litter and debris everywhere. For a country that has such obvious natural beauty it was astounding how careless the locals were. Is it poverty? Does poverty mean you can't afford to care? From my ivory tower in the west it is easy to say and criticise, but there are some basic things that could be done such as not throwing things in what are largely considered across Nepal and India as holy waterways. The river I was looking at, the Bishnumati, or the beloved river of Lord Vishnu, was disgusting emitting a putrid smell and was a rather unwholesome greeny brown.

It is no surprise that Nepal is a target for both Indian and Chinese investments, trying to encourage infrastructure projects and moderninsations that are desperately needed. Yet the politics of the fractured communities and castes from different backgrounds both religious and ethnic in the aftermath of the civil war means that the country cannot agree on any policy, which coupled with the institutional corruption endemic in the nations upper echelons means that it is developing much slower than it needs and is stuck in a status quo. The place did very much feel like a melting pot between the two colossal powers, with the population's appearance being a mix of Indian, Mongoloid and Tibetan as well as the tell-tale tower blocks and goods of China. Architecturally outside of the old town the rest of the city didn't have the same energy or feel, I wondered if I would have the same experience as I traveled to different parts of the city or country or if Kathmandu was a bubble distinct to the rest of the nation as so many capitals are - I would of course see.

After following the main road over the river, the white and gold stupa of the monkey temple came into view perched on a hilltop.

As I approached, I exited the more residential streets to what was certainly a busier area with cars and mopeds zooming by and street children nipping the heels of passersby. As heart breaking as it is, I just had to ignore them, of course this was after first saying 'namaste', I would then walk on. It was so hard to just move through them and not feel anything, however I didn't want to encourage the harassment. There is also the issue of encouraging those that choose 'begging' and preying on tourists to pay for their existence, often via gangs exploiting the young and vulnerable, taking advantage of soft-hearted emotional tourists. It is important to add that not everyone you encounter that is asking for help is calculating or that ruthless, as sure as the day is long there are those that are genuine in their suffering. For me, seeing the urchins in their dirty, ragged clothing and with dusty, unkempt, un-brushed hair with patches of dirt on their faces I could not imagine they were actors performing a role, and I felt nothing but shame as I navigated my way through the gathering throng assuredly indifferent to their plight.

I crossed the road deeper into the swell, what made the experience harder was that they spoke English, there was a clear way to communicate and therefore unlike other parts of the world it was impossible to screen out the chatter as simple white noise. As cries of 'my mother is sick' and 'I am so hungry' are directed at you, you can't ignore the fact that this person is talking to you. After wading through I spotted a little old lady who held her hands in a prayer like gesture, my heart melted and I placed a few notes in her hand, not much. Immediately I was swarmed.

A couple of routes lead up to the temple, I decided on the eastern way straight up via many aged and steep stone steps. Rhesus macaques were everywhere – hence the colloquial name of 'Monkey Temple.' Heading up there were many friezes, tablets, statues, shrines and depictions of Buddha, as there are all over the country. The Buddha was born in the south of Nepal in a place called Lumbini about 2500 years ago around 500BC. Not really a God himself and with Buddhism not really a religion, Gautama Buddha can be considered more of a sage or mystic that taught a revolutionary form of philosophy that by its teaching sought a higher mind which in essence is the elevating of oneself above the concept of suffering and the taints of emotions such as lust and hate to achieve the ultimate of nirvana and enlightenment. At a time when Ancient Greece was just reaching its classical phase and still looking to the pantheon of Olympian gods, to talk of self-improvement and the removal of deity worship really was a radical concept, hence his lasting impression.

Alongside the various images and depictions of Buddha there were a variety of Hindu figures, the most prevalent being the image of the elephant like Lord Ganesh. In truth, Ganesh is a pan-Hindu God, insomuch as Hinduism itself is a fusion of various concepts and beliefs, which much like Buddhism talks of a Dharma or way of life, hence the comfortable melding of the two belief systems. Ganesh is the remover of obstacles as well as the patron of arts and science at the same time as being identified as the God of beginnings – a very multi-talented fellow!

This blending of Hinduism and Buddhism in Nepal is seamless and upon just surface reading it is clear how many similarities there are between the two belief systems, this was always affirmed by whoever I spoke with on the subject. Apparently, it was the Victorian Brits that 'lumped' all these beliefs, notably the vast array of 'Hindu' strands together under one heading, not fully understanding them and thence coining the name Hindu for this plethora of deific worship in the region.

Walking up the steps with my small ruck sack I found it tough going, I didn't think that Kathmandu was that elevated and the route up although steep was nothing more than I was used to at home. However, I certainly didn't feel great with my lungs and legs burning, hopefully this was just some post travel lethargy.

At the entrance to the top I paid my 200R (about 1.25 GBP) which was a foreigner price, for locals it was 50R. Some foreigners complain about this external vs internal pricing. I have experienced this a lot on my travels from China to Ghana and I am all for it. Coming from a nation that I know to be privileged, how could me paying a little more making very little difference to me if it meant a local who lives on very little can enjoy the same thing is surely not a bad thing. Gladly I handed over my inflated price and made my way up the final steps slightly sweaty and out of breath. If this was how I was feeling on this small hill, it was nothing much more than that, then I had a long way to go physically before base camp and not a lot of time to get there. Passing through the archway to the plateau I was met by a spectacular view of Swayambhunath stupa.

A stupa is typically a mound-like or hemispherical structure containing relics that are used as a place of meditation, Swayambhunath itself was white with a gold chimney like spire with the eye of the Buddha painted on its four sides. Prayer flags had been tied to almost every available point and seemed to dot the skyline. I shared the space around this magnificent structure with several tourists, pilgrims and traders. I sat on a wall for a time watching the locals go around and round with their circumambulations spinning prayer wheels as they went sending their message to their god, it was a fascinating if somewhat incomprehensible sight to someone who does not share their beliefs. Then again, I thought it was essentially the equivalent of a Catholic using a rosary to pray which I am sure they too might find odd. Either way, one couldn't help but have a profound respect for these pilgrims as they single-mindedly went about their business.

The whole area, although thronging with people and animals (dogs, monkeys and birds) had a sense of peace and calm. The locals failed to react when the mischievous macaques would steal an orange or plastic bottle before running off and scaling the many brick buildings. Watching the monkeys swing about and climb all over these holy shrines dangling from prayer flags made me chuckle, Nepali's are seemingly extremely tolerant, barely batting an eyelid at these simian trespassers.

Looking at the buildings surrounding the stupa the effect of the earthquake in 2015 was only too apparent. The stupa itself was only superficially damaged but the rest of the buildings were far less fortunate, some were visible wrecks or piles of tumbled bricks. Sections of the stupa area had been sectioned off for being too dangerous and in one corner there was a large sign thanking the people and government of Hong Kong for their aid and assistance with restorations of a particularly important mural that had been all but destroyed. Again, it was clear that Nepal was in desperate need of investment (and aid). One likes to think that as well as external aid, the people of Nepal would also see their heritage in these buildings and the structures as part of a shared history, one that was of the utmost importance to preserve; and yet across the city and on the peak surrounding the Monkey temple, the evidence of this attitude to shrines, temples and building of a bygone era was definitely lacking. I saw traders throwing rubbish in corners and making no effort to be respectful of what was clearly a holy place, one gentleman in particular was leaning lethargically on a small waist high shrine to Buddha whilst smoking. The place was crumbling in no small part due to the devastating earthquake, but this coupled with the lack of a sense of preservation or care means that without proper action, these majestic icons of years gone will slowly crumble into ruin, as was happening before our eyes, apart from the odd apparent external aid program eagerly trying to swim against the tide of decline.

This is at odds with my experience of most western countries, who look to preserve everything taking pride in any monument, building or place of interest. In Nepal it is as if you are living in the past, history abounds everywhere; it is refreshing to have access to the tangible past as a traveller to literally feel hundreds if not thousands of years of history under your feet and fingertips, but at the same time it is also quite sad as the years of use and general wear and tear means these fantastic examples of human endeavour are but moments from destruction at any given time. I pondered the dichotomy of this, but thought, then again aren't we all but a moment from that?

I wandered to the rear side of the stupa where several shops were selling their wares to tourists. I was specifically interested in the masks of Buddha and Ganesh. After a recent trip to Mexico I had bought some Mayan masks and had done the same on previous trips over the years, it was obviously becoming a thing to me. At this stage in my trip I had no intention to buy despite the rather decent $10 price quoted. After a time talking, laughing and general convivial conversation the shop owners whole demeanour changed as I made it clear due to this being the start of my adventure I was in no position to make a purchase, he didn't understand the concept of browsing and was quite angry that I had wasted his time; "always English people!" he exclaimed as I exited the shop. I couldn't understand this mentality, he had spoiled any chance he had of me returning later, which wasn't wholly unlikely as this was a beautiful view and I had a month. (In fact, I did actually return in my last days, not to his shop however!) I couldn't help but smile as I left, acutely aware that he makes a living and that time with me chatting was time he could have been fishing and hooking other potential customers, but no one should be coerced or feel compelled to buy something. It was a shame also as I had quite enjoyed the chat about living through the earthquake, its effects and what it had meant to him and his business. Part of me really wanted to return at the end of my journey, to remind him who I was and then do my souvenir shopping to dispel his obviously less than positive view of the English, then again as one swallow does not make a summer, one positive instance of an Englishman would probably do little to affect a lifetime of views. I turned the northern corner and looked over my shoulder to see him still muttering away angrily to himself and gesticulating, I genuinely couldn't understand what I had done to wind this guy up – I thought we had had a good chat, a bad day perhaps.

The view from the stupa across Kathmandu was awe inspiring and it was the first time I had really looked at the city. What first caught me was its apparent size and dimensions, spreading out from where I was on the very western edge to the east as far as the eye could see, and yet it wasn't tall and imposing. A big 'small' city comprising of some million inhabitants, not a particularly large number of people as far as global capitals go, positively tiny considering it is the capital of Nepal which itself is over 27 million – a surprisingly small portion in comparison. There was a grey/brown haze to the skyline just hovering above the cityscape, a clear effect of pollution and smog. Having walked the largely untarmacked, potholed and stone dotted roads and alleys bustling with cars, bikes and bicycles I could see where large amounts of the dust had come from as there did not seem to be much in terms of heavy industry. I was already feeling the itch of a cough in the back of my throat; I would be using my 'buff' over the next few days to act as a mask whilst I walked the city. Next, I was struck by both the multicoloured buildings and the lack of anything over around 5 storeys. In all it didn't seem like a typical capital city, with no particular points of interest on the skyline, the hill I was on was probably the closest thing to it. I was aware the smog might have made the distance I was seeing not quite as far as I thought, but that being said, it was still quite unspectacular. There was very little to complain about though, the vibrancy of the coloured buildings and sounds of life emanating from the city up to the hill were enticing, I could not wait to explore more.

Before that however, it was nice to just sit perched on the top beside Swayambhunath stupa soaking in the atmosphere and letting the world go by around me. The playful macaques were causing havoc and the pilgrims circling the stupa were non-stop, it was the perfect place to just 'be'. After a while tiredness seemed to catch up with me, just 'being' can be quite tiring, so decided it was time to head back to the guest house. En route I bought a bottle of water and practiced my very limited Nepali (how much, hello, thank you, good-bye,) the lady and her child had great fun laughing at my shoddy attempts, it was all in good humour though. On the road I stopped for dinner which consisted of fried rice and a buttered naan, both insanely big portions and at the time delicious. However, as I walked away the lingering aftertaste of garlic hit me. I have a slight intolerance to garlic which is a nightmare in a country like Nepal that uses garlic extremely liberally as it is widely believed to aid acclimatisation to altitude. The next morning, I was struggling with phlegm and a sore throat. Last stop before bed was a little shop just across the way from my alley, I purchased a local beer called Everest (which was surprisingly good) and pack of Oreos to munch on as settled down to read tucked into bed listening to the rains lashing down.

Day 3 - Kathmandu

29/2/2016

I eventually dragged myself out of bed around 8:30am, I had been awake since 3:15am and hadn't been able to settle, thank God for the British History Podcast – well recommended, it would be my constant companion over my time in Nepal.

I headed to reception to change money and discuss my early morning check out the next day as I was heading to Lukla and the Himalayan range. Whilst standing at the counter I again looked over to the large poster on the wall that offered trips around Nepal, to Bhutan and even Tibet. My mind whizzed at the possibilities wishing I could do it all.

The exchange rate for dollars to the rupee was about 100/1. An easy cross calculation which was nice.

The transfer was arranged for the following morning about 5:00am by private car back to the airport for my flight to the mountains. It is possible to hike to Lukla from a place called Jiri, it takes between 5 and 7 days depending on the individual. I had considered this, but seeing as there was so much else I wanted to cram in my time it was best to get straight to Lukla, being the gateway to the national park and trail to Everest Base Camp (EBC).

My experience of times and scheduling in the country thus far had taught me to be cautious, I hoped they were going to be reliable for the pickup and on time as the flight was leaving about 6:30am so would leave little room for error. As for my Bhutan enquiry Duran, the owner, was trying to get me to commit to a 5-day trip. This would be far too long based on what time I had available and far too expensive as the going rate for any foreigner (excluding Indian nationals) in Bhutan was $250 per day, although this would include a private guide, car, accommodation and food it still feels like a lot when booking. I settled on 3 days and 2 nights knowing this would be just enough to see some of the essentials such as the mountainside monastery near Paro and the capital, Thimphu. Date wise I decided the 20th/21st/22nd of March, this would give me 20 days to make it to Everest Base Camp and back which by all accounts would have been extremely conservative as the relaxed schedules only take around 16 days. I might also have a few days on the return to see more of the city and possibly even shoot off to somewhere else for a couple of days. That would all have to wait though, I had the trek to EBC to contend with first. I arranged to meet Duran at lunch to visit the agent and go through the formalities of the paperwork and visas as well pay the bill.

Positively bouncing at the prospect of the trip I headed out into the city for brekkie and then onwards to Durbar Square – Bhutan, wow.

Durbar Square, which literally means 'Royal Square' sits in front of the palace of the old Kathmandu kingdom and is one of three palaces in the Kathmandu Valley, the others being Patan, that I would visit, and Bhaktapur. The buildings consisted of courtyards and temples and are a showcase of the local Newar design, the Newar being the historical people of the Kathmandu Valley

To get to the square from where I was, I had to head southwest from the guest house. With my camera out I was hoping to get a feel for the old town and the area. After a few 'twisty turny' alleys I entered a small square with a stupa in the middle. There was a group of children running around and playing with a hacky sack and a school sandwiched between two buildings in a rather out of the way fashion. "Is this Durbar Square?" I ventured, "YES!" was the unequivocal response as they all giggled and laughed. I had seen a few pictures of the square so knew this was not it, but thought asking that rather than 'Am I near?' would be easier if their English was ropey, clearly it was ropey or they were playing with me, the smiles, giggles and twinkling eyes told me they were having me on. I smiled back kicking the sack as it was lobbed in my direction to cheers of encouragement and made my way across the small square still heading in what I was guesstimating was the right way

Strolling by I passed my art student friend from the day before, Rajesh. Today he was with a female traveler, we walked semi side by side a short way and I heard the same patter he had used with me, apparently the square with the stupa was where he worked in a students' art shop, I had noticed a little shop in the corner but hadn't gone further to investigate. So, this was the way they hooked tourists, using the old 'art student' story. No doubt he was a struggling artist (being generous,) but his 'gallery' from I had seen was less of an art installation and more of a typical tourist shop. It is a shame they feel the need to use these tactics to get you to their shops or to buy something, but I guess competition is rife and everyone is struggling to make a living. Plus looking at the 'artworks' they are nothing more than tourist prints, and Rajesh is but one of a team of salespeople trying to drum up business, probably for commission. I smiled and moved on as I heard the conversation taking similar directions to my own.

That morning I had been stopped several times already over the short time I had been wandering about. I was beginning to feel a little fed up and impatient of the pestering, but was determined to be nice, so a few deep breaths to remember that they are just trying to do their jobs and that it was a very thankless task and I carried on, keeping up with my 'I'm sorry' and 'I just want to walk alone'

I hadn't noticed a build-up but suddenly there seemed to be a lot more traffic as well as what were clearly tourists and groups; even at the relatively early time of 9:30am. After running the gauntlet gently urging my way between the throng to what seemed the busiest corner, I guessed I had found the way to the square. I stood in front of a ticket station where I paid my 1000R to be able to enter Durbar Square. Again, much like Swayambhunath stupa this is only payable by tourists and is quite considerable compared to the general costs of things. Though it is essential for the upkeep and preservation of this World Heritage site that suffered enormous damage a few years back when the earthquake struck on the 25th April 2015. One hopes that some of this revenue would be going towards the much-needed restoration and rebuilding, then again in Nepal with government corruption rife who knows. The ticket, although initially only for the day of purchase can be extended to cover the period of your stay in Nepal if you provide a passport photo, a silly system but quite nice to allow the ticket to be extended for a longer stay, especially as the square has so much to offer. The ticket officer who served me was wearing a uniform much like an army uniform.

As I entered the square person after person kept coming up to me offering their services as a guide, I realised that you have to walk around purposefully looking like someone who knows what they are doing otherwise you are just a sitting duck. I looked across the square at the numerous magnificent buildings literally being propped up by posts of wood on all four sides and at all angles. Some of the buildings had signs saying to keep out and keep off as they were too dangerous, visibly they looked on the verge of collapse. The local people and animals seemed to view these signs as purely advisory as they lounged about on the crumbling structures and cracked stone-works. It was so sad to see these clearly fantastic buildings holding on for dear life staying standing only with the help of carefully placed props to quite obviously prevent what looked to be their inevitable demise.

Maybe I had been a little hasty talking about how decrepit and crumbling Kathmandu was. I spoke to one of the numerous vendors and he explained what the earthquake had been like and what I was looking at was the aftermath, very little had been done since by way of rebuilding. He believed it would take years to take Nepal anywhere near back to where it was, if indeed at all based on Nepal's meagre financial capabilities and economy. He feared Nepal would never be the same again and he was probably right, though in some ways maybe it would not be all bad and may provide an opportunity. It all depends on your point of view and your vision. The vendor carried on to explain how over a 24 hour period the shaking had ebbed and flowed culminating in a massive 8Mw quake on the moment scale literally bringing structures to the ground in piles of rubble killing thousands (official death toll 9000 souls) and making huge swathes of the city unsafe. He told me how after months the area where we were standing, an ancient brick paved pathway and square, seemed to float on the ground beneath as the land took time to settle. He and his family had had to leave their family home which was now in ruin to live in a tent in a 'tent city' set up for the homeless on the edge of town. Officials were still in the process of working their way around the city giving their sign off as to whether buildings were safe of habitable. If the building was condemned, as had happened to the vendor, then the family would be left with nothing and unfortunately the government were in no position to offer help, hence the tented accommodation and the reliance on foreign aid and charity. For the vendor and his family, they had a very uncertain future, and they were not alone.

There were green shoots that Nepal was rebuilding, especially in areas around the centrally located palace, not so much in Durbar Square, and the green shoots were very early and probably not growing at the rate the city and country really needs. The wounds will heal in time no doubt, but the scars will be forever.

What astonished me as I wandered about and spoke to the odd person was to see how people were so accepting of their situation. I can't imagine how these families who have lost absolutely everything would survive and recover without financial aid or a robust social welfare system, how lucky we are in the UK. These families thought of nothing beyond the here and now, and despite obvious hardship still offered a warm smile and a welcoming 'namaste'. Incredible.

Despite so many of the buildings in Durbar Square not being safe to enter with ropes and tapes covering the entrances, the vision of the pagodas was extremely impressive. I think the hope that the (relatively) steep entrance fee would help in some way to regenerate the area absolutely justified the cost.

Before I left the square area, I had wanted to try to catch a glimpse of the living god, the Kumari Chok on the south side of the square. This is a young girl, chosen through an ancient selection process proving her to be the reincarnation of the Hindu Mother Goddess, Durga. Her role was simply to make public appearances to allow the followers to worship her. The requirement of an entry fee put me off a little, making a business of divinity. Everyone needs to make a living (I guess) and I didn't fancy trying to engage a guide having managed to brush off most that had tried to attach themselves to me on my way round, plus there was a huge crowd around the small entranceway. I would try another time if the opportunity arose.

At the south end of the square was a coffee shop that claimed to be the first coffee shop in Nepal, the lonely Planet had written this also. I tried a Himalayan Java that for 110R was lovely (I completely recognise the craziness that I thought nothing of paying 110R for a coffee but initially baulked at the 1000R for the entrance ticket. Considering an average meal was 10-15R, this coffee was extortionate.) The taste was incredibly strong – my heart was literally beating out of my chest! Looking out of the window sipping the heart quickening coffee, Durbar Square struck me as genuinely one of the world's most stunning places truly deserving of its place on the heritage lists, though the square has been devastated by the earthquake this does not diminish its amazing beauty, in a weird way it almost enhances its charm, adding another element to its character. I do hope that one day they manage to repair some of the more affected structures, though I don't think it is essential and the place still has tremendous appeal. A Chinese couple were having wedding pictures taken amongst the wrecks and between the ruins (and pigeons), they didn't seem too bothered by the destruction.

Finishing up, I decided I would come back at the end of the trip to have a wander around again (I didn't), and then made my way to book the Bhutan trip. Initially on meeting the manager of the travel shop he told me to return a bit later as the agency was closed for lunch. I was eager to settle my plans, but this didn't bother me, any more time to wander about this incredible place was welcome. I chatted to another guy who was also staying at my guesthouse. He was an older Norwegian gentleman who walked with a limp. He shared some very interesting stories about his travels in Thailand and the Gambia and was quite interesting if a little strange, he wanted to go out to the villages for some reason but was unwell so had to wait in the guesthouse until he was better. I couldn't establish what was wrong with him or why he wanted to go to the villages. As he didn't offer the information I didn't want to pry, how typically British of me.

The Travel Agent was down a back alley that didn't initially fill me with confidence, tucked away behind a hotel. Entering, the office was all wood paneled and seemed very dated, very '80s' with pictures of the destinations one could arrange trips to on the back wall. They seemed to not like my dates and wanted me to go for longer espousing all the lines like 'you won't have enough time', I assumed this was patter for tourists, which although I completely agree you can't see a country in three days, I hardly imagine an extra day would make any difference, I knew what I wanted to do and three days was sufficient for me and what I intended to see. We waited about 45 minutes as the rep was trying to call the tourist line of the Bhutanese government, but no one was picking up, he was getting visibly frustrated, I didn't mind. As we sat, I was beginning to waver on my dates but not being sure about Everest Base Camp and how long my trek would take me I didn't want to commit to something that I would regret later.

Eventually he got through and we settled days and dates, the 18th March to the 21st which was 3 nights and 4 days, all for the hefty price of $1200, a huge amount for the time I would have, solely due to the $250 cost for being in Bhutan per day, however this was truly a magnificent once in a lifetime opportunity and one likely I would never have again. Using my credit card, he swiped it in the old-fashioned way with the carbon paper backing, no contactless here. I chuckled and smiled, which he returned hearing my thoughts. Next, he took my passport to be able to obtain my visa, I am always unsure of handing this over in foreign countries, but he assured me I would have it returned in time for my flight the next day. In terms of itinerary I was ultimately flexible knowing that mostly I just wanted to see the Tigers Nest monastery and Thimpu the capital. I would receive my itinerary in the next few days via email and he would go ahead and arrange my visa. That was it, everything was settled, I was going to Bhutan. Just the small issue of getting to EBC and back...weather permitting. Next stop, Lukla!

Day 4 - Kathmandu to Lukla

1/3/2016

What a terrible sleep.

I got into bed around 10:00pm knowing that I had an early start – 4:45am. Almost every hour on the hour I was waking up to check my watch and see the clock creeping forward. I was struggling with a blocked sinus and had the hint of a headache, I was starting to see why so many people talked about acute mountain sickness (AMS) mania, every time you are short of breath or have a 'heady' feeling you start to attribute it to AMS, you even start looking for symptoms and imagine things that aren't there (Mark Moxon discussed this in his travel diary about Annapurna, a really good read, as are all his diaries.) I had a lack of appetite, thumping headache and what seemed to be an element of insomnia – not so much AMS as the closet hypochondriac in me creeping out. I popped a 'Piriton' pill praying it was only a combination of the dust, pollution and garlic laced meal that brought out my symptoms and took an Ibuprofen in preparation for the doubling of elevation I would encounter that day. Supposedly this would help combat any swelling and reduce any headache; it was advised by many as a short-term measure for altitude acclimatisation.

By 3:30am I had an hour to burn, I was so excited the possibility of actually going back to sleep was impossible. I was feeling pretty rough mind you but was trying to put this to the back of my mind, it couldn't be AMS could it? I was only 1600m up and had only just begun my journey, what would I be like at 3500m?

My taxi was late, I wasn't surprised though. One thing I have come to appreciate whilst on the road is that my nature for absurdly specific time keeping at home and in general everyday life is nigh on impossible in other countries, waiting a day for a car in the middle of Ghana taught me the lesson of patience that I have kept to this day, you quite honestly have to just go with it and be confident that things always turn out alright – trying to ignore that I had a plane to catch I sat patiently in the reception. The night porter who had been in a sleeping bag on the reception floor (incredibly friendly, even though I had openly disturbed his sleep) jumped up and made a few phone calls, one of which I was to find out later was to the owner who I am sure was delighted to be woken at 4:45am. As we both started to worry where my ride was a taxi crept its way up the alley pulling to a stop just outside and a sleepy guy who had clearly only just got out of bed emerged.

For this time of the morning the journey was surprisingly eventful. The driver seemed to speed up at the craters (it would be an understatement to refer to them as just pot-holes) apparently in the hope that the car might not crash into them but glide over, this was not the case, although the suspension held up impressively well considering the absolute battering it was taking. These cars were pretty durable I had to admit. There were several near misses with locals even though the sun had not yet risen as they meandered across the streets in their all black ensembles, they looked without a care in the world as we flew past within mere inches, my driver seemed to not even blink, a natural race driver if I met one.

We entered the airport via a checkpoint, I was reminded how old the airport looked, as if from a bygone era, and that era clearly didn't have to worry about threats of terrorism, security was astonishingly lax at a time where in the UK we are stopped and body scanned by guards more than once. Here the same occurred in theory, but by a team of people that had a 'I am only doing this because I have to' way. In fact, no one actually took much interest in my passport or me, just my air ticket.

I waited in a large area with a surprising amount of local people. I hadn't expected so many to be travelling to the mountains let alone with all the goods and things, however once through to the boarding area I realized there were a number of small flights crisscrossing the country all via small 20 seater planes. As expected, there wasn't a large domestic market. The flight I would be taking with Yeti Airlines was a twin propeller number for tourists and porters only.

Unfortunately for me, the flight was delayed by half an hour almost immediately. I had read about the quick change in the weather meaning that many flights were often cancelled so times were often just a guideline. Lukla, where we were headed was so high up in the mountains, flights to and from are often affected. It was a little foggy in Kathmandu (KTM) this morning but that was more to do with the temperature change as the sun rose heating up the air and ground quickly, so I guessed the fog meant the weather was not great in Lukla.

Eventually, closer to an hour after planned departure we were ushered into what I can only describe was a prison transport for the mere yards to the strip and the plane. Upon seeing the plane for the first time in the flesh I was amazed to see its size, it was absolutely tiny making the stories of crashes all the more real, I could easily imagine this small piece of metal flying into the mountainside caught in thunder and storms that frequented the mountain ranges. The engines were laughably small and to hear them reminded me of a moped running at full tilt, not powerful enough and always on the edge of overload and breaking down. The dawning on me of the fragility of this plane was sobering; one always imagines airplanes as hulking great machines, these looked barely serviceable. A couple sat next to me and discussed that not two weeks before there had been a crash in Nepal, although this flight had been from Pokhara, Nepal's second city, they made everyone on board grimly aware of the extremely ropey aviation record in the country – cheers guys!

We sat on the runway for what felt like an eternity, the pilot and co-pilot were both locals and wore cool leather flight jackets like something from 'Top Gun'. The cockpit had the usual nobs and buttons and yet it did not look modern, but rather like a cockpit from the 1930s, it was an antique. I wondered what the mileage of the thing was; it felt like a hand me down from fifty years ago. It was old. Looking out the window I was just below a wing, I wondered, in the event of a crash, was this a good place to be? The engine was deafening and the rotors span at invisibly quick speeds. We edged forward slowly before ramping up speed rising quite effortlessly into the fog/polluted sky of KTM headed on a bearing northeast for Sagarmartha.

I got my first real glimpse of the Himalayas in the distance as we rose above the cloud line, everyone had their cameras out, me included. Over the next 30 or so minutes of the flight the mountains just kept getting bigger and bigger. It was breathtaking, a magnificent sight I could never tire of.

Butterflies leapt in my stomach as the plane dipped sharply, the mountain ranges were lost behind the walls of the valley we were descending into, which would be my last view of the range for a few days until I was well into my trek.

Lukla airstrip was tiny and unlike any I have seen before, thankfully from my vantage point I couldn't see clearly until we had landed. The strip was on a slope steadily rising making the full use of gravity to slow the landing planes as quickly as possible due to the extremely limited landing zone, ingenious but terrifying. Throughout the flight there had been a bit of turbulence, but one would imagine that is par for the course on these types of flights and in a weird way made it more memorable. As the door opened, I was more than relieved to be back on terra firma.

I was met by a porter for the lodge I had arranged to stay at, the Lama Guest House, his name was Lama. He offered to take my bag but in typical James Joyce fashion and despite feeling terrible I refused. My ears were now gone, and my head was throbbing intensely. Lama offered me a tour of Lukla (I would later find it was a rather small place with a few alleys and offshoots, it really is in the mountains!) I explained I was feeling a bit rough and thought a nap was necessary to help re-acclimatise my body to this new environment, he completely understood, and we went to check in and get me a quick breakfast.

Lukla was stunning with green trees and a mystical fog; it was a world away from KTM and just how I imagined. The buildings were like alpine timber lodges with bits hewn from local stone, hand carved as opposed to kilned bricks – it was beautiful. The guesthouse was on the main throughway of the town and built upon three floors, it was timber built and creaked with every step, there was the aroma of wood, cooking stoves, perfume and a mustiness of sweaty bodies combining to unblock my nasal passages. As I sat on a padded bench alone, I was the only guest today (it was just before the season began so just before the rush) I devoured a breakfast that consisted of a bowl of thick porridge, strong black coffee, plain omelette and a pancake leaving me stuffed, it was simple but superb.

The walk from the landing strip had me feeling the altitude of 2800 metres. I was glad I had decided to spend a day in Lukla before moving on, although originally I had planned for two days to ready myself before setting off I thought it might be better to bank a spare day for further on the trail just in case, that was if I woke not feeling too 'heady' after only one days acclimatisation.

With my belly absolutely bursting I unzipped my sleeping bag and slid in, I was in a room with two 'beds', really, they were just wooden benches with a thin cover. I slept from 8:00am to 4:00pm without stirring. I took another Ibuprofen and Piriton when I woke and headed out for a wander. I chatted with Lama a little bit and he told me that a guide was unnecessary to base if I was confident and managed the altitude. This had been my hunch all along, especially as there were villages every few miles on the trail if I needed to stop or had any emergencies. He also gave me some sage advice as an experienced man in the mountains, he suggested I didn't stick with my intention to stay in Phakding, as this was at a lower elevation than Lukla and would not aid my acclimatisation, he suggested I push on to Monjo which was at the same as Lukla at 2800 metres.

Leaving my electronics to charge I went out. Charging was going to be a constant hassle throughout the trek as electricity is largely limited by the hydro-capacity, which is less in the winter until the waters unfreeze and with the general availability of generators. This coupled with the reality that due to the cold the items would discharge very quickly meaning that each day I would be having to pay the equivalent of 2GBP to charge, not an exorbitant amount but something that westerners don't really consider when they bring their iPad, iPod, iPhone and cameras for company.

The first stop on my tour of Lukla was Starbucks – yes STARBUCKS! They also had an Irish Pub, a Scottish themed Highland bar, as well as North Face, Mammut and other branded shops, not authentic I might add. Lukla was very quiet as I strolled around and the only foreigners I saw were like me, enjoying a Himalayan latte, a coffee with delicious sweet honey.

I headed back and had a huge plate of vegetable noodles for tea and decided to tuck in early with a book.

One note on the Lama Lodge, there are numerous alternatives in Lukla to stay and they all look equally nice so tourists could comfortably stay in any of them. However, Lama Lodge was the only one on Booking.Com which made me feel at ease booking through a reputable site, although this was not necessary serendipity struck as the people were lovely and the rustic lodge had everything I needed. I would have been interested if in high season it would be possible to just book on arrival, this I was unsure of and the sheer volume of traffic on my way back to Lukla suggested that booking ahead was advisable.

Day 5 – Lukla (2840m) to Monjo (2840m)

2/3/2016

A supposed early start became 9:00am.

I had had a nagging feeling overnight that I wasn't carrying enough cash, the whole trail pretty much was cash only apart from Namche Bazaar, a place that was about a third of the way to EBC. It wasn't that I didn't have enough, on the one hand I was sure I did, but it was that just in case scenario, when travelling I always think to add up my budget of what I think it should cost, then add 20%.

The small bank in Lukla wasn't opening until 9:30am, although the times I had already discovered were flexible so knew not to 'bank' on it exactly, pardon the pun. After finally getting into the bank about 9:20am, early, I went back for a breakfast that consisted of porridge and coffee after which I repacked my bag and then leisurely made my way to the TIMS registration point.

TIMS stands for Trekkers Information Management System, a rather nifty way that the government and tourist bureau try to keep tabs on people wandering in their wilderness, with checkpoints at various points of popular trails. It's quite a sensible thing that we have to register upon joining the trails, not only to ensure that you have a permit and paid your fees, but also so they know your intended route and duration, fundamentally for safety. Of course you can do whatever you like once on the trail within reason, but the fact that so many solo travellers had disappeared over the years highlighted that in spite of the trail being safe as far as hiking and these types of expeditions go, there are still dangers for independent trekkers. At the office there were posters of missing people from around the world, it was an eye opener especially for a solo traveller like myself, however I was in no doubt of either my ability or my intentions to do this alone. I pondered the question when he asked duration, initially I had thought 18 days and intended to go at a really comfortable pace enjoying the scenery stopping as and when I felt like it. This had now become 16 days in my mind, until some locals suggested this also might be too slow. As I stood at the TIMS checkpoint I gave the number 15 days but decided there and then that all decisions will be dictated by how I felt physically, to come this far and to have to turn back because I hadn't paced myself or had rushed a day or so quicker was unthinkable, I was sure that the altitude effect would be an obvious barometer of what I should be doing, so the key was to listen to whatever my body was telling me.

As I prepared to set off on the trail I was still feeling a little rough but the mania regarding the AMS had begun to wane, my condition was a combination of factors, no doubt altitude was contributing but more likely it was due to the jet lag and smog. The last question the TIMS officer asked me was whether I had an iPad or iPhone – this struck me as a little odd, were there robberies? Was it market research?

After a rather convivial chat, I wish the guard farewell and waved goodbye setting off on the trail. It was a cool morning with a clear azure blue sky and the odd cotton wool cloud; it was beautiful. The road was clear with not a soul in site, time for a Grand Adventure!

There was an archway that delineated the boundary to Sagarmatha National Park. I stopped to take a picture before positively bouncing down the stone/dirt path descending into the valley beyond.

After no more than 10 minutes a Korean guy caught up with me, his name was Sun Jun Park. He asked if I minded if he joined me, my immediate feeling was that I really wanted to do this alone. I can be a bit of a loner at times and really had no intention of spending time with someone else, in fact I wanted time to be alone. But then the superstition in me reared its head, maybe it was a sign that neither of us should be doing this alone? I decided to take it as it came. I smiled and said of course shrugging off my initial reservations and we set off, side by side.

The first topic of conversation were our plans for our respective treks. Jun's English was very good, and even though we had to work around certain vocabulary it was amazing what we could cover with a bit of patience and time; and boy did we cover it, the trip, families, sport, politics, the indomitable spirit of communication - amazing.

From the outset I was very clear about how I was going to tackle the trip, so it was really a case of whether Jun wanted to join me. I explained each of my stops and the reasoning behind it i.e. duration, elevation and of course altitude. Jun himself had literally jumped off the plane in KTH the day before and had come straight to Lukla to start the trail without even a day to acclimatise, in either KTH or Lukla. He was from Seoul, which at only about 30m above sea level meant that even KTH was 1400m above what he was used to. The jump immediately then to Lukla at 2860m was not advisable and I suggested he turn back and spend the night in the town knowing that the effects of altitude may take a few hours to really hit. He dismissed this idea telling me he had tablets, I wasn't convinced but he seemed happy enough, so we trod on.

It was no wonder Jun wanted to walk with a partner seeing his lack of preparation and knowledge of the trail apart from a book he had borrowed from his local library about the world's best hiking trips. I was sure I was going to be of help to him, despite my novice status as I tend to read a lot and am such a thorough planner.

Jun told me that he didn't have much money as they had blocked his card when he had tried to use it in Kathmandu. My first question was why had he rushed to the mountains where likely he would have no phone access nor bank access for the duration of most if not all the trail? He seemed surprised at this and hadn't considered that. I explained to Jun that Namche Bazaar had a bank, ATM and access to an international phone which was the next major waypoint on our journey a couple of days away. He was happy with this, deciding to deal with the problem then. This highlighted a real difference between Jun and I, if our initial conversations hadn't suggested it, this certainly did. If I had been in his boat I would have waited in Kathmandu even if it meant a delay on my expedition to ensure I was in the best place to complete it. Preparation. Jun on the other hand seemed to be very much in the 'winging it' mode, certainly not my way of doing things; I accept things don't always go as planned, but with proper planning I always feel ready for most eventualities and in any event have thought through possibilities. 'To fail to prepare is to prepare to fail,' Sun Tzu, The Art of War c500 BC.

We followed the trail towards Phakding, sat at 2600m this had been the proposed night stop before I had spoken to

Lama at the guesthouse. The original proposal followed the walk high, sleep low mantra to help combat the altitude sickness, it was about pushing your limit before backing off for the night. However, Monjo was now the destination at 2800m metres and the same elevation as Lukla, even though it was further and meant a much longer day of 9 miles (14.5km) on a very up and down, uneven and stony path. The extra benefit was that the next day would be less of a slog cutting the distance to Namche Bazaar to 5 hours. I had been warned that the route between Monjo and Namche was particularly arduous. I hadn't really considered the importance of this, but if the way to Namche Bazaar was going to be mostly uphill including some quite steep trails up to the 3440m, taking some of that strain when we felt fresh today was not a bad thing. It was amazing how in only a couple of days I had started to become so aware of time on feet and elevation as opposed to distance as the weight we were carrying, the terrain and the elevation were such important variables that to say we were walking 8-12 miles is not enough to convey the challenge we faced each day.

Time and distance generally passed swiftly underfoot, and conversation flowed freely. Jun was 24 and had just graduated from a Firefighting Academy in Seoul. He enjoyed football and socialising and this trip, like mine was a sort of pilgrimage for him before he went home to embark on his adult life and career. I explained my journey was also for the challenge and a sort of bridging moment between two parts of my life, before I too had to get on with the 'grown up' stuff. I didn't go into further details regarding the spiritual motivations for the trip, he both might not understand or care, and to be honest I wanted to keep this private.

We passed through villages and settlements of only a few buildings, such as Cheplung (2660m) and Ghat (2492m). There was stunning scenery of blue skies, mountains, running water and farms of stone buildings, with the odd prayer wheel, shrine or prayer flag dotted about, it was like some Himalayan fantasy, as if someone had reached into my mind and plucked out my exact impression of the Himalaya.

The road continued (I say road, but there were no cars, so it was more like a path, interchanging between dirt, cobbles and stone) with only minor ups and downs. Both our bags were already starting to feel heavy, but we were in positive moods and neither were in too much discomfort. We both had packed over the ideal amount in weight, bearing in mind the time each day we would be carrying them, my pack was close to 16kg. I had intentionally packed light from the UK and had left items at the guest house in Kathmandu, so despite the weight being over the suggested 14kg, I wasn't too much over. Jun's' on the other hand was a lot heavier, I had a feeling this might cause him some trouble later. Mine was a concern for me and yet it felt significantly lighter than his He supposed it was somewhere between 18kg and 20kg, yes, I thought, the higher end for sure.

Before long we approached Phakding and decided to stop and have a break, Jun wanted to press on, but I was eager for a coffee and to rest up, it was a marathon not a sprint I told myself.

We met a Swedish woman on her way down with her guide and a Thai couple that had studied in the UK who were being paid to write a blog and already were having one published about their experience on the Trans-Siberian Express, they were fascinating (check out PakaPrich on Facebook). Both groups had porters and guides and seemed surprised when we had said we were going it alone. I had pored over maps of the trail and read all I could, I was sure that the route was very straightforward, the only issue was carrying packs and managing the weight and altitude. I knew if I could manage this, as much as one could, I would be fine. Even arranging accommodation on the fly as it were, was not that difficult seeing as we had joined the trail in low season, we had our pick of the places to stay. Carrying the pack I knew would be tiring, having set out a few years previously on the West Highland Way in Scotland before giving up a few hours later due to the weight of my pack I was more than aware what the impact of carrying too much weight over an extended period can do. Being realistic about your capability at the start when you are fresh and energized is key. At 16 kg I was comfortable that I could carry it the times and distances required, although there were indeed times throughout when I certainly wished I had had a porter.

The trail up to this point had been scenic with the constant sound of the flowing Dudh Koshi river, meandering through the valley below which we were following. Upon leaving Phakding the feeling of comfort quickly changed as the way got increasingly difficult at every turn. We were still heading north but had now entered a dense forest and the route had taken on slippery dusty trail on a significant incline making it very hard going. Map distances seemed to have spread out and time was passing interminably slow as we ambled along step by step. It was purported to only take 2/3 hours from Phakding to Mondjo, we were almost 2 hours out from Phakding before there were any signs of life, first at Toktok and then Benkar (2905m.) We met a couple of guys coming down the other way, an American and a Brit. They said it had taken only a couple of days for them to descend from Base Camp. They warned us of foods on the trail, especially eating meats as they had both suffered dodgy stomachs. I imagine that seeing as everything must be carried up from Lukla, foods are not or might not always be the freshest. I had tended to mostly take vegetarian options already but thanked them for their advice which supported my thinking.

Both mine and Jun's backs were starting to ache with the bags digging into our shoulders, mine was feeling far heavier than the 16kg I knew it to be, Jun's must have felt horrific. It had been a long day and our bodies were telling us they wanted to rest.

The final thirty minutes into Mondjo was hell and a real eye opener of what we had to look forward to as steep stone steps kept dotting the route, the return would be lovely I thought but right now this was not really helping. I don't think either of us had thought it would be this tough this early on, I don't think it was a conditioning issue, I think it was the bag. What had we let ourselves in for and what was next?

The run up to Mondjo was also hampered by having to constantly stop to let past trains of Yaks and donkeys. We were unable to get into a rhythm which was probably adding to our discomfort. I watched the fiftieth batch of Yak traipse past admiring their tenacity, these amazing creatures were absolutely fearless, wandering along the trails with huge loads where the footing could be quite unsteady and crossing the massive wire and steel bridges without pause that spanned the valley and the raging river below, each following the one in front. They were smart too, often you would see a train of yak pass with the shepherd way in the back harrying the stragglers. They knew where they were going and kept on regardless. As the yaks approached it was important to move out of the way as though they are docile, they are so large and extremely powerful that any bump could easily send one careening of the edge. Because of this, it was important to keep to the inside and not towards the edge as the yaks passed. For the umpteenth time I scrambled up the scree and waited for them to pass.

Just before Mondjo there was another cable bridge, but this one was far larger than any we had encountered yet. They had all been equally terrifying as they swayed with every step and gust of wind with only wire suspension an inch thick to holding us above the river and rocks tens of feet below. Every time I felt unsure or uncomfortable, I would think back to watching the yaks crossing and reassured myself that if ten to fifteen of these beasts could cross at one time, then my bag and I were no problem. As I crossed, I remembered reading about Sir Edmund Hilary back in the early 1950s and wondered how he would have traversed these truly massive stretches of fast running water. Trekking to base camp let alone climbing would have been a very different proposition back then.

The first structures of Mondjo that popped up on the horizon were reminiscent of ski lodges in the Alps, the only difference being the multicoloured prayer flags that dotted the landscape tied to buildings, trees and bushes. These flags are an ever present wherever you travel in Nepal as well as the prayer wheels.

The first place turned out to be a guest house, so we went in and asked for a room, Jun wanted Wi-Fi. They had rooms but no Wi-Fi, so we moved on to the next place a little further on, this one also had no Wi-Fi. Apparently, it was down more often than not which explained why I had been unable to get online in Lukla that morning. A shame as I had been unable to tell anyone back home that I was setting off. I had prepared Glaiza that contact would be limited but had not really expected there to be no way of communicating. Up in the Himalayas, even in this day and age, contact with the outside can be difficult.

Our room was 300R which was shared between us and had a private shower/toilet. The room had two beds either side of a window and was much like the room in Lukla in that it was essentially a bench. This was the norm throughout the trek, which after a day hiking didn't matter in the slightest, it was flat and that was enough. I managed to jump in the shower and get a little hot water, Jun however waited as he wasn't feeling so good and so missed his chance as a travel group of Brits arrived who must have all had the same thought, exhausting the of lukewarm water. Hot water comes at a premium in the mountains as it all must be boiled, including shower water. They have solar heaters on the roofs to supposedly generate the warm water, this is extremely limited though and invariably showers are at best room temperature, though more likely 'fresh.' Hot showers are so unheard of they must be jumped on (or in) when the opportunity arrives.

The British group that arrived were from a company called Exodus Travel who were doing a 16-day trip costing £2000 excluding flights. A tad expensive but not as much as I thought and clearly, they were well taken care of. The common answer for why people were doing it with the group as opposed to alone was the ease of arrangement and security. I understood, but my trip had come in a lot less and I don't think I missed out on anything or took any unnecessary risks, plus I had the luxury of going at my own pace. Everyone is different though and having met the guide and looked at what was on offer, it wasn't extortionate.

Jun and I slid into our sleeping bags about 5:30pm very tired and a little achy. We had enjoyed a dinner of the local dish, Dhal Bat, and strong coffee. We were soon fast asleep with neither of us waking until 7:00am the next day.

Day 6 - Mondjo (2840m) – Namche Bazaar (3440m)

3/3/2016,

My body hurt! From the noises coming from the cocoon on the bed next to me through the night, Jun was hurting too.

We went for breakfast and it seemed the whole guest house was on the move; people rise early here I thought as I checked my watch, it was a little after 7:00am. I had another omelette, this would become my breakfast of choice, and a lovely flat hard Tibetan bread. I really was happy that we had decided to stay in Mondjo, the tail end of the trek yesterday was all uphill and would have proved an exhausting start to today had we left from Phakding.

At the edge of Mondjo we passed another checkpoint, this time for Sagarmatha National Park itself via a grand archway, a portal that led down to the banks of the crystal-clear river, fast moving in parts, running between tree lined slopes surrounded by snowcapped mountains all around, I had never seen views like it, simply stunning.

As we took in the wonderful vistas yaks and Sherpas passed us carrying ridiculously large loads. The Sherpas navigated the rutted and potholed trail with such ease never misplacing a step, like mountain goats in their element be it on the path or clinging to a slope as a herd of yaks passed.

The environment was indescribably beautiful; at one point we passed three humongous footbridges, all in quick succession zigzagging the river. They were like something from Indiana Jones and the Temple of Doom, you know that bit where he cuts the rope and the bad guys fall from a tremendous height into the raging torrent below. Except in our case, the bridges were made of steel and there were no crazed priests of Kali chasing to cut out our hearts!

The first hour of what was meant to be a 3- or 4-hour trek passed very comfortably. We both had slight niggles and aches from the previous day but neither of us were suffering any apparent altitude effects, which was a good thing as we were intending to head higher. I was feeling pretty good.

After crossing the bridges, the path plunged back down to the riverbed, and we found ourselves walking where the river ought to be. In this area the river was running light, in a matter of weeks the water would rise again making travellers have to hug the sides of the hillsides, from where we were traipsing along the pebbled riverbed I couldn't see where the 'actual' path should be.

The path then rose again on the right-hand side of the river and we had to stop again as we approached another broad footbridge. There was a pair of Sherpas who were carrying packs, the size of which I could barely imagine. They looked so cumbersome and the sheer dimensions would have made walking the up and down trails agony on the back and the knees. Both guys were far smaller and much younger than me at 24 and 16 years of age. We sat down on some of the larger boulders and I shared a trekking bar and some water with them. They were appreciative but clearly didn't want to linger, for them time was indeed money, so they waved goodbye and pressed ahead. The Sherpas travel between the villages and base camp, they move as quickly to their destination as they can, as that is where and when they are paid, by weight. Hence the stupidly heavy packs they carried, the more they did the more they would earn.

As we checked the map, it looked like Namche Bazaar was not far over another bridge, I hadn't paid too much attention to the gradient and so 'not too far' turned out to be not entirely true and became a monster two hour slog uphill giving me my first true experience of the effects of the altitude on the body, this was definitely not mania. It is remarkable how quickly the it really hits and how it affects you. All of a sudden, my leg muscles were burning, and my heart was beating like it was going to burst from my chest. We pushed on for 30 minutes but had to keep breaking. I couldn't believe the sudden onset and worried at the intensity of the symptoms, at this relatively low altitude, what would the effect be higher up?

We both discussed how we were feeling, for me it was absolute fatigue, physical exhaustion but not much more, I expected a day in Namche Bazaar would help me acclimatize. Jun on the other hand had both my fatigue as well as a thumping headache. He hoped this was a residual effect of any jet lag, but in my heart, I knew it was that he had come up to this elevation too quickly, for him a rest day in Namche Bazaar was essential.

After another particularly difficult stretch the path reached a small plateau area with an amazing view of the snowcapped peaks in the distance. I enjoyed seeing my first site of the titans before sitting down for a drink of water. Jun had lain himself out with his eyes closed, he was visibly struggling. A German group arrived. I don't speak German, but I caught the word 'Everest' as well as the gestures and gathered they were saying to each other that 'you can see Everest' from here. The group rushed over to where we were and started taking photos over my shoulders. Not only had I not realised that the particularly black topped mountain on the horizon was Everest, but I had sat down with my back to it! I quickly stood and turned around and lo and behold, now I had been told I could make out the famous form that was the dark fish tailed peak of Everest. The range became immediately more beautiful, what I was seeing was Chomolungma, the Mother Goddess of the Universe in Tibetan, and she looked so tantalisingly close. In reality, the mountain was still several days walk away, but now we had seen her in the flesh, the goal to reach her was something tangible. 'We might as well go home then' I quipped; everyone laughed politely, I'm sure everyone says this. We packed up and moved off with a newfound vigour, at least I did.

Back on the trail, a man came towards me with a small backpack wearing jeans, a local. I wished him 'namaste' and we stopped for a quick chat, I wanted to know how much farther to Mondjo. He said we still had about two hours to Namche Bazaar, that struck me as quite far, especially comparing to what it looked like on the map. The timings and distances we were given by people varied wildly and so made it hard to judge what was real, as in reality the time depended on how quickly you went, and this was different for all people; relying on times and distances was a bit hit and miss as it was dependent on the individual. The local was on his way to Lukla and eager to press on, so we said goodbye and we ourselves carried on to our destination. Jun was visibly deflated at the prospect of so much farther to go, he was not enjoying himself.

Seeing Everest had spurred me on in spite of the way I was feeling. Continuing to Namche Bazaar was solidly an uphill walk through trees and dirt paths dotted with roots sticking out of the ground. The altitude was really hurting us both now, and Jun was looking in utter agony, his steps were slow and clumsy, and he walked with his eyes closed. I kept looking over my shoulder at him as although my body was screaming at me to stop through tiredness my head wasn't hurting, the effects of altitude are really a personal thing and it really does affect everyone differently, which is why it is so important to take it steady over the first few days you go over your natural altitude and especially over 2500m. Jun was saying he felt sleepy and had flu/cold like symptoms, this was a sure sign of acute mountain sickness (AMS) so I told him he had a choice, either descend or get to Namche Bazaar and we could go from there. He wanted the latter but at times he seemed completely unable to make to it. Seeing someone suffer AMS in front of you makes you even more aware of the need to be cautious going forwards.

The final stretch became a fog of continuing forwards and upward steps. The stops to catch our breath became more and more frequent and every time we would start again after a few steps we were breathless and both looking to the other for another break. I had done a fair bit of exercise before the trip and was relatively happy with my level of cardiovascular fitness so couldn't understand how hard I was finding this, even allowing for my pack. I started to wonder if other people suffered the same and was immediately reminded of people trekking without packs and the value of that as a few people appeared to skip past us. Determined I pushed on, Jun just followed silently, even though it was only day 2 of the trek I was having doubts as to if Jun could really accomplish this, the way I was feeling I was even questioning myself.

With complete relief we came to the next TIMS checkpoint that pointed out the entrance to Namche Bazaar, a beautiful picturesque Himalayan town. The location was absolutely stunning with a view that was something out of a dream as clouds were rolling in which would later become fog due to how low they were (or how high we were, I couldn't tell.) The sun still shone, and it was quite warm when walking in it, much like a typical early spring day in England. It was amazing to see so many people living their lives so far away from a city or town, and so high up, so shut off; remote. There are no roads or cars in Namche Bazaar and the nearest big town was a day's walk *and* flight away. Everything had to be brought in either by foot or helicopter which explained the higher food and drink costs. A meal in Namche Bazaar was as expensive as a night's stay at 300R to 400R which was equivalent to roughly £2 to £3. Namche Bazaar has a bank, a Post Office and even a few ATMs and is essentially a functioning town, albeit a very small one, with all the typical amenities including restaurants, hotels and schools, except it is built into a Himalayan mountain valley, with walls sloping upwards from the entrance we came in much like a bowl. Walking up and down daily must mean these people are fit as a fiddle with incredible cardiovascular levels, it's all stairs and slopes at 3440m. I wondered how older people would cope.

We decided to stay at the Khumbu Lodge that sat high up in the centre of the town for $3 a night, which included a shared common bathroom. Completely exhausted we settled in, I decided I would take a rest day the next day to help acclimatization as the walk from Mondjo had proved far harder than I had expected. I didn't want to risk any further symptoms of AMS if I could help it, and if a rest day would help then there was no rush. I would not be completely idle though, I would have a wander and go up a few hundred metres and come back down, again to combat any AMS. I suggested Jun do the same, initially he wanted to push on, then said he would sleep the day, I said he should see how he felt after a night's sleep. Jun was not in a good way; I had seen him deteriorate to the point that I didn't think he could go any further. I hoped he would not push himself too hard.

Lying down in my sleeping bag it was again early evening, I had a little time to read and relax. There was still no Wi-Fi, so I sent a hugely expensive text to Glaiza to let her know I was safe. Before long I had fallen into a deep sleep.

Day 7 - Namche Bazaar (3440m) – Khumjung (3780m) – Namche Bazaar (3440m)

4/3/2016

For the acclimatization trek I decided to head up to the Khumbu region, the famous homeland of the Sherpas, the centre of which is a small town called Khumjung. This town has a school dedicated to Sir Edmund Hilary, the first man to summit Everest with his personal Sherpa, Tenzing Norgay, the national hero of Nepal.

In the night I had heard Jun's breathing which was very fast and again in the morning he had complained of a headache and was sleepy. I was seeing before me the effect of not taking altitude seriously, he had come up so fast from Seoul to Kathmandu and then straight up to Lukla his body was screaming for a break and telling him he needed to go back down. I had had a couple of days in Kathmandu and then a day in Lukla before setting out and was not feeling 'tip-top' myself. I urged him at a minimum to stay in bed and rest if he was determined not to head back the way we had come. I even proposed, much as I didn't really want to, that we stayed another day to ensure he had adequate time to get himself right. Although I hadn't planned to do this trip with him at this stage I had a 'no man left behind' mentality and wanted to make sure if I was going to make it he would too, he had been good company and was a great guy to boot. If he couldn't manage this himself, I would do all I could to help. The fact he was struggling so badly at such an early point however was ringing alarm bells. Altitude is such an individual issue, there is still little understanding as to why some are affected more than others, all you can do is prepare as best you can and ascend little by little so your body can adjust, by coming straight up into the range Jun had really not given himself a chance. Looking at me through half closed eyes with a grey/white pallor he said that if he was going to stand any chance he needed to go up higher and return to Namche Bazaar, that only by going up and down might he feel better, I couldn't argue with this logic.

We quickly got our bits together and set off up to the Khumbu region and the village of Khumjung just north of where we were. I was quite looking forward to the excursion, we weren't time bound and in a rush to get anywhere in particular and had a view of Everest to look forward to at the grand and apparently overpriced Everest Lodge which sat perched on the crest of the mountain we were on – of course, views were always weather permitting.

After a delicious breakfast of porridge and an omelette we headed northwest back up and out of the bowl that was Namche Bazaar on the circuitous route I had mapped out taking us through Khumjung and back. We weren't carrying full packs which was a nice change, although I decided to take a small bag with water, a jumper and a few bits; it was a bit chilly in the morning and as we were going higher I wasn't sure if the temperature would dip and so I didn't want to risk getting sick, I already had a runny nose that was proving to be a pain in the bum, I wasn't sure if it was hay-fever (I don't normally suffer) or something to do with altitude. I was constantly blowing my nose and snorting out my nasal passages which was fortunately keeping the build-up of pressure and headache at bay. Contrary to how tired I had been the night before, and much unlike my companion, I felt quite strong and fully recovered.

The way out of Namche zigzagged up the hillside on man-made stone and pebble tracks, the ascent and paths rose quickly. It was quite disheartening to see children, adults and the elderly appearing to move up and down the same byways with apparent ease, with barely a grimace, as we slowly but steadily made our way. This route we were following was also the way we would head to Tengboche, the next stop on the journey, so it was nice to get a feel for where we were going and a heads up of the way.

As we reached the edge of the village we were met by a fabulous view of the Khumbu range of mountains as the sun was still rising bathing the snow topped peaks in yellows and oranges, it was energizing; at least for me it was, Jun however was barely taking anything in.

It was only about 9;00am, but the Namche Bazaar seemed alive with locals and Sherpas. I said hello or 'Namaste' literally a hundred times, this never got tiring though, the Nepali people of this region were incredibly friendly, even those under the weight of some 40kg mammoth pack they always managed a smile, genuine or not, some acknowledgement without breaking stride or losing balance. This friendliness and encouragement was so welcoming and comforting, I never felt isolated.

Straight out of the town we stumbled upon Syangboche Airport, the closest airstrip to EBC which was on a relatively (but not quite) flat space suitable for only short take off aircraft and helicopters. I remembered reading that it was now only used for dropping in supplies and rescuing the injured mountaineers although had historically been used to service guests at the Hotel Everest and those wishing to skip the picturesque but strenuous trek from Lukla. The jump in altitude had proved too much for most being at over 3000m meaning most guests immediately required oxygen and invariably suffered AMS symptoms, so the strip was used less and less frequently to the point that the 'Airport' now mostly only seemed to see the odd Yak or walker on a day to day basis.

The environs reminded me of Exmoor or the Yorkshire Dales with wide open undulating hills of scrub and grass blowing in the wind and surprisingly few trees considering the dense forests we had already walked through since Lukla

The views from the Everest Lodge, a short distance from the air strip, were spellbinding, the vast size of mountains was humbling, they seemed only touching distance away which belied the actual gap between us. Sadly, as expected Everest herself eluded me behind a curtain of fog. We followed the path around the back of the Lodge and then around the edge of the mountain itself on a track roughly three feet wide. At times it felt like one was only a few feet from certain death, we were so high up and the drop so sheer, the reality of falling would have meant undoubtedly one wouldn't survive. Sobering. Those with a fear of heights stay well clear. From here I had my first sight of snow, melting in the mid-morning sun. The transition in the environment had been almost imperceptible from the dusty bowl of Namche Bazaar to the spring like grassy hillsides with a smattering of snow. Jun was now happy and seemed to be a bit brighter, who could fail to smile when surrounded by such majesty.

The path descended again into the valley bringing the village of Khumjung into view. No sooner had we entered the vicinity than a smiling old man came across to me clearly intent on talking, I smiled and waved as I approached to bridge the gap between us. He told me in surprisingly good English that in 1977 and 1997 he had sherpa'd up to Camp 2 on Everest, 6400m up! He had been a cook for an expedition and from his apparent good health there was no question as to his fitness, he laughed that now he was too old to go again, much to his sadness. The local people of the mountains are incredibly hardy and phenomenally fit wandering up and down the hills at such altitudes from such a young age. Looking at Jun his smile dipped, he could see Jun struggling trudging behind me, I asked about the effect of altitude on him and the other locals. The old man nodded sagely, the locals also have these problems, nobody is immune to the effects of the altitude, though he prescribed one remedy that always lessened the pain, go slower. He laughed to himself. He believed that we as foreigners do not work hard enough to temper our speed and thinks this is a critical factor in the acclimatization process, we trek to EBC much as we live our lives, far too fast! He suggested we take our time and enjoy his home before rushing on up the trail. Taking a moment to think, it seemed such an obvious observation as I saw locals walking about (less so the Sherpas), they all seemed to go at barely much more than a slow amble. Sensible. The slower you go the less demand there is for the body to circulate what little oxygen there is. I was going to take this on board, and would encourage Jun to do the same, looking at him though I didn't think he had it in him to go much faster.

Khumjung village was much like Namche Bazaar in many respects, in that it was built into the hillside with buildings dotted rather haphazardly, some, one storey others two. There was also the constant white noise of fluttering prayer flags in the incessant breeze that blew through the valley. Everywhere you looked, tied to every available place were reds, greens, blues, pinks and yellows. The individual properties were separated by waist high stone walls that were neither bricked nor packed earth but rather stacked, they seemed little more than demarcation lines not even fit for holding back the wandering herds.

We walked towards the centre of the village and then on towards the school, the Hillary school, dedicated to Sir Edmund built by his Himalayan trust in the 1960s which now served over 350 children from primary to secondary levels.

I asked a young man nearby where we could buy water and he kindly showed the way as not many people were around. He too was a Sherpa and had also been to Camp 2 this year, however next year he would go to the South Col at around 7900m. This is a camp, usually camp 4, below the peak and at a pass between Everest and the nearby mountain Lhotse. The young man was clearly fit, but I was surprised at his size. He was going to have to carry some large weights up the mountain and I wandered how he might be able considering his frame; at around 5 feet 6 inches and not particularly stocky. His credentials of Camp 2 however told me enough, this guy was tough.

Leaving us the man literally hopped and skipped up a stone stepped path that rose back up our side of the valley to the other side which led past the airstrip and back to Namche Bazaar. I marveled at this Himalayan gazelle, or mountain goat to use a local animal.

Jun and I went to carry on but he was not good, at times he would slump on boulders and shut his eyes, I couldn't really imagine the internal battle he was fighting but he certainly didn't look great and in spite of his constant profession of being okay, he clearly wasn't. I felt between a rock and a hard place. At this point I didn't think Jun should continue up the trail, that further altitude would do him no good, and his already painful symptoms would only get worse. I told his as much and he nodded but told me he wanted to continue. I was in no place to force him not to continue, I urged him in the strongest terms to reconsider carrying on the next day and that an extra day, possibly re-running this trek would benefit him. He was adamant he wanted to continue but conceded we would review in the morning. I didn't want to argue, so left the conversation there, we continued past the school along the path the young man had skipped minutes earlier, we two wanderers however were far from skipping.

As we came back down into Namche Bazaar I felt better for the ascent and was surprised to see the town transformed, on every available flat space there were bright orange tents being erected for the upcoming groups and expeditions to use for the climbing season. It was clear to me now that this was why there had been so many Sherpas on the trail, carrying equipment in preparation for the many groups imminent arrivals, the sheer volume of traffic and people that would be coming to the region meant lots of food, stoves, tents and camping gear amongst many other things were now needed at various stages all the way up to the peak of Everest, especially as those summiting would likely be spending in excess of 6 weeks camped at the base acclimatising before hopefully achieving that magnificent feat. I stopped to look and take pictures; Jun had his head down and just wanted to get to bed and so ploughed on to the guest house.

I went down to a pharmacy to get some pain killers for Jun as he had almost run out. When I got back, we chatted and for the first time he admitted "bro, I don't think I can make it." As sad as it was, I think he was finally being honest with himself. He was quite emotional, so I suggested he rest and we get up more leisurely the next day before we made any concrete plans.

AMS is so strange, I had felt very little discomfort so far. The next day was a big day for Jun, either he would wait, turn back, or, what was most unlikely to me at this stage, go up another 450m. Looking at the route and elevation on the map, I didn't expect the next day to be easy for either of us.

Day 8 - Namche Bazaar (3440m) to Tengboche (3870m)

5/3/2016

I wrote this account some two days after the event as this day and the day after were quite eventful, the journey to Tengboche being particularly challenging. I can't put my finger on why though, although I can hazard a guess, we were on our feet much longer than we should have been carrying our packs uphill, not helping any AMS symptoms or tiredness we were already feeling. The guidebooks say this journey should have taken around four and a half hours; we were very wide of the mark entering Tengboche some 7 hours after setting off!

I got up not long after 6:00am, having stirred far earlier but not really wanting to physically raise my tired body. We had breakfast, the usual eggs and porridge, and then made our way leisurely up the route we had taken the day before towards Khumjung. However, this time upon reaching Everest Lodge, instead of heading past and over the hill we turned east on a path that wrapped itself around clinging to the side of the valley. Once we had descended slightly, the way was a relatively flat dust track which made the going quite easy, if the whole way up to EBC would be like this, it wouldn't be half as bad as we had anticipated.

We passed a stupa dedicated to Tenzing Norgay which had spectacular views of the surrounding area, from the vantage point we could pretty much see the whole route we would take to Tengboche, it didn't look too far away in the distance but sat perched at the top of the mountain range facing us about 10km as the crow flew, but likely farther due to the quite substantial elevation. I was eager to get moving to get the adrenalin and muscles pumping and shake off any fatigue and lactic build up from the day before, looking over I could see Jun had spied the settlement also, his face falling as he saw a) how far it was and b) the climb that looked to be up ahead. It was evident he was not feeling up to it.

For a short time as we walked in the morning sun (it really was quite warm) and for a period joined by an Indian mother with her 10-year-old daughter and her 14-year-old friend. It was the daughters dream to climb Everest, or so her mother said, her daughter looked miserable trudging along begrudgingly. I got the feeling this was more of a pushy parent thing as she looked absolutely miserable. The 14-year-old however was positively bouncing skipping along, she proudly stated how she was going to climb Everest this season and before going on to try and climb the 7 summits in the region, being in her hopes the first and youngest Indian girl to achieve such a feat, I applauded her bravery and drive, inspiring.

Before long, it was clear our pace (or at least my pace) was quicker than them, so we said our goodbyes and left them behind just as the mountains seemed to envelop us, encroaching on the trail. The sheer size dwarfed what we had seen previously, and I now felt we were in the thick of it. The landscape was like one from a 'Lord of the Rings' film, with running rivers and snow-capped peaks with sheer forested sides.

A little further on, at a place called Sanasa, a Nepali guy we had met on the first day with his mother called over to us, he owned a guest house on the route. Jun had some garlic soup to help with his AMS symptoms, though in my opinion the advice to consume as much garlic as possible had done little more than elicit an interesting fragrance from my Korean friend, doing very little to alleviate the actual symptoms. I was given a free coffee. Our hosts English was excellent, and we chatted about all things as Jun slowly and quietly had his soup, he was really not enjoying this and seemed to be a world away lost in thought. Eventually we had to leave but I said if the chance arose, I would stay over on my way back, he wished us a safe journey and we departed.

Leaving Sanasa the path dropped dramatically by a couple of hundred metres at Phunki Tenga to 3250m, this was a good thing for Jun's head and our lungs, but not our knees and legs that now burned and throbbed with the impacts of the descent. As we leveled out, I had a rather depressing thought that as much as it was nice to have descended, we would be heading back up via a final stretch that consisted of a 700m incline that would or should take around two hours.

The bridge at Phunki Tenga was the beginning of this final stretch to Tengboche, a winding trail snaking up the mountainside, so Jun and I decided to stop for a break. This was a mistake as neither of us was physically feeling good, the weight on our backs had never felt heavier and Jun was struggling to the point that he wasn't talking, was bent over and only shuffling forwards. The bridge itself was a huge steel suspension structure spanning a wide part of the river with a restaurant at one end. I bought a coke for the sugar hit. The river was raging against the stone, boulders and rubble below. It was a magical place to just sit and watch the world and soak up the atmosphere, reminding me of where we were, and how lucky we were to be there.

This feeling quickly dissipated as the time to press on came, and so reluctantly we crossed the bridge to head up to Tengboche. As we had stopped so often over the morning, we were already pushing four hours. My legs and back were sore but apart from this I was feeling okay and was eager to get the day done. Jun however appeared like a dead man walking, in my mind it was clear he should have stayed in Namche Bazaar, at least, but there had been no telling him. As we began up the trail I felt my stomach growling, I hadn't eaten at Sanasa as I wasn't hungry from breakfast and had only just grabbed a Coke at the restaurant by the bridge, how I regretted that with the relatively tough gradient in front of me. For the next three hours we wound our way up through a dusty forest weaving between the trees and boulders that lined the way over uneven ground. From the beginning every person we passed said it was only two hours, literally everyone, even after an hour! At one stage someone said twenty minutes feeding us completely false hope. Very quickly we got into a semi-routine where we would stop every twenty or so yards so Jun could lean on one of the boulders and just hang his head breathing deeply. I would wait and walk back to him; check he was okay and encourage him to press on. This was increasing my workload making me tire faster too, but I knew that if he was too stubborn to turn back, I had to get him to Tengboche so he could eat and rest.

Eventually, at a snail's pace I passed a pile of the holy stones under a line of prayer flags to enter the town of Tengboche. Jun had agony etched on his face, following me on auto pilot barely looking up from his feet as he swayed from left to right with each step forwards. The journey had taken far longer than we had anticipated and due to the dust mixed with our sweat I had never felt so unclean. I was determined to have a shower and so paid the equivalent of a night's stay for a bucket of warm water and washed outside. Due to the fall in temperature the water got cold rapidly but it was lovely washing off the dirt. I knew it was unlikely I would shower again on the trip to EBC, which Jun did point out to me, in essence arguing that washing was a bit pointless, however after the tough day such small luxuries made a big psychological difference; there was no harm in delaying the filth. I savoured the feel of the water on my body and quickly got redressed as snow began to fall. It was a beautiful sight as I stood looking out over Tengboche. A small mountain village that was developed around an ancient monastery wrapped in a thickening fog on a canvas of fading light and steadily falling snow. It was a moment that will live with me forever.

I had already seen a dramatic shift in the environment since Lukla, and the next day would see another dramatic change in the landscape as the increased altitude meant that the trees would thin out for a more boulder-strewn landscape and far less foliage. One of the joys of this kind of trip is the physical journey through the different climate zones and experiencing that subtle and slow shift from environment to environment. Despite my fatigue I was looking forward to pushing on.

As we arranged rooms hello's and hi's were said to people that we had met going back as far as the first day on the trail, this included the Thai couple, a Canadian group and the Indians. I sat and chatted for a while before heading to bed around 7:00pm. Jun was already fast asleep. I slept like a baby before awaking at 5:30am the next day.

Day 9 – Tengboche (3870m) to Dingboche (4410m)

6/3/2016

I could hear scrabbling in the wall behind my head, it hadn't been the best night in the world, despite being tired, and the noise of mice (or rats) scurrying about mere inches from my head made it difficult to settle. Lying a bit askew I massaged my back, it was in bits from the previous day, I just hadn't been able to get the pack to sit right, especially later after a few hours up and down hill. Packing a bag is a science.

Jun and I hadn't yet decided whether to stay another day in Tengboche, although we had discussed it, it was dependent on how Jun was feeling. With hindsight this was the best course of action for both of us, a day to acclimatise, wander and rest would have made the final few days trekking a lot easier, but he was eager and indeed adamant to move on saying when he woke he felt a lot better. I was sure this was either bravado or a false dawn, sadly it was the latter and he was to regret this choice. I looked out the window and grabbed my camera, Tengboche in the morning as the sun rose was just breathtaking, seeing the dawn light reflect off the monastery and the glistening morning snow was incredible especially with the mountains as a backdrop. I just stood taking in the moment, Tengboche was so beautiful, it was a shame my visit was to be so short. This idyllic hamlet in the Himalaya's was exactly what I had come to region for.

After breakfast we were on our way, a pack of dogs followed us down the hill as we walked past the old monastery towards a tree line in the distance. The canines followed us all the way out of town barking the whole way, clearly exerting their authority. Dogs aren't well treated in Nepal and if they all behaved like these mongrels I could see why!

The road dipped as we headed northwards into a magical rhododendron forest, the rhododendron being the national flower of Nepal. It wasn't quite time for their flowering, but the walk itself was still very pretty, and as we walked in silence, the stillness in the air was contemplative with only the sounds of crunching snow and debris underfoot and rustling leaves as snow fell to the ground, I imagined myself in C.S Lewis's famous Narnia.

The path broke out from the forest to a valley where the way now hugged the slope next to the river and was extremely narrow, this made the going slow especially with the numbers of Yak passing the other way. At one point I even put on my crampons as the way was so icy, it was actually a little dangerous, but we didn't stop to consider that fact and just pushed on as quickly as we dared. The river below was running with quite some velocity, smashing into rocks sending up spray in all directions. The sounds of water and the smells of the forest made a comforting companion as we started to climb quite steeply back out of the valley to a new landscape of scrub, bush and sand. It was incredible how quickly this transformation could happen, within a matter of moments.

We had our first break at a place called Pangboche which was about a third of the way to our next destination, Dingboche. No sooner had we set off again, Jun was requesting that we stopped for lunch, he had been putting on a brave face, but I could see the AMS symptoms were back and giving him grief. We carried on a little while before he called a stop at Shomare where we ate a lunch of Dhal Bhat with a lovely Dutch couple, it was great to chat. Diomoxin came into the conversation, being one of the drugs used to prevent and help with altitude sickness, as well as the positives and negatives of it. Dehydration and loss of taste seemed to be the biggies for those guys, I myself had decided I wouldn't take it and would use my time ahead of the trek and rest days to manage any symptoms, I wasn't in a rush. Jun and I agreed he probably should have done the same – so he decided in the unlikely event we were to come across a pharmacy he would get some Diomoxin – though we both knew that once the symptoms were already upon you it was probably too late to do anything about it with the only choice being descent, for Jun that bird had flown.

We set off again and quickly started heading markedly uphill higher into the mountain range. Everywhere we looked and on every part of the hillside there were stone walls parceling out the land like back in Khumjung encircling innumerable Yaks, much like cattle farms back home, the difference being a vastly different scenery. Whilst walking I met a man from Dingboche, he was a lodge owner and offered us a free room for the night, this was very kind – although rooms were cheaper than food up at this height freebies are always good. The benefit to the guest house for this kind of offer was that a guest would need food and water, the bed was secondary.

Signs of landslides and rock falls were everywhere we walked and, in some cases, cut across our paths. It was slightly disconcerting making us more cautious as we went, a constant reminder that nature here was wild and although the weather was being kind, the tempestuous winters could be lethal. Boulders as big as cars littered the area, some looked entirely out of place sat in the middle of fields completely on their own, how did they get there?!?

My back started hurting again but was nothing too serious if I went slowly and kept a good posture, Jun on the other hand was stumbling from rock to rock for support again. If I didn't keep stopping, I would have been out of sight quite quickly.

As we walked over a bridge which spanned the Khumbu Kola stream, we stepped into what appeared a kind of desert and this stayed the same all the way to Dingboche, we appeared to have entered a new climate zone. It was a lot warmer than Tengboche, despite the increased elevation and a lot drier and dustier. At this stage we had been going for 7 hours 15 minutes, on a journey that should have taken around 4.5 to 5 hours. I thought maybe they didn't include breaks, of which we had had a few, and that it didn't factor in trekkers carrying bags, or AMS symptoms like Jun.

Entering Dingboche, to both our surprise there was a pharmacy at one of the guest houses, maybe we shouldn't have been so shocked as up here, more than most areas, it was essential to have access to medications, especially pills for altitude. The lady in the pharmacy suggested he take some Diomoxin and dutifully sold him a batch of 10 for 450R – they wouldn't last long, the idea is to use them as you acclimatise, so she also advised he not go any higher for 24 hours at least, preferably 48.

We passed some Sherpas that we had been passing on and off since the second day and they gave some advice for the next stage of the trek and where to stay; they suggested staying in Dingboche for a rest day and then head straight to Lobuche as opposed to stopping in Dughla that was the next intended stop, this would mean a longer days walk, but being rested should mean we should have the energy, also the guest houses here were lovely and the place seemed pleasant enough. I thought it was as good a plan as any.

Settling into our guest house and our free room Jun went straight to sleep. As I lay in my sleeping bag, I thought through the number of options we had in front of us, all however were dependent on how Jun was feeling. It felt odd to now be doing the trip with him in mind as I had intended to go alone, but now we were a pair. I knew without me he would struggle to go any farther, if indeed he were able to at all, he was not in a good way if the raspy snores emanating from his cocoon were anything to go by.

There was no Wi-Fi in Dingboche nor signal for phones, so I decided to charge my electronic items, have some famous EBC trail apple pie and settle in with a book.

Day 10 - Dingboche (4410m) – Rest Day

7/3/2016

I didn't manage either cake or reading the night before as I had my first bout of AMS, a dry throat, short breath and a runny nose. Jun bless him was almost in tears with the pain and needed to vomit, I was sure he wouldn't be able to go any further, but we decided we would give him some rest to give him the best chance of being able to proceed, now would be the best time for a rest day and was make or break for his journey.

We went for a short walk after breakfast, he didn't look or feel great so after a call of nature and a quick chat about football I left him sleeping and went in hunt of coffee and some apple pie – it is famed in Nepal as being a widely available treat on the trail and of being a relatively good standard. As usual I had been charging my bits as in the cold the batteries tend to drain very quickly and, in some cases, just die. My iPod charged but my iPad didn't which was odd, fortunately I still had around 80% which would definitely see me through for a couple of days. As I was leaving, I wrapped both in my sleeping bag hoping they wouldn't drain, there is no central heating in the guest houses, so the rooms tended to get cold.

I went back to the pharmacy where they had given Jun pills the day before, out of the corner of my eye I saw large plates of cakes and that they served coffee, upon request I was told there was no coffee but the cake was delicious, and not because I had had few luxuries this high up on the trail – the apple pie was genuinely superb. The lady who served me was the same who had helped Jun the day before and after asking about him suggested an O2 saturation check, this is essentially a pulse check to see how much oxygen is in the blood. That made sense as it would give a clear indication of where he was and a final decision on his likely ability to proceed. I said I would send him down later - we checked mine and it came back about 82% which is fine considering the altitude, although long term at this level is not advised when normal is above 90%. My resting heart rate was about 80bpm which again, at this altitude was fine, and although slightly above the norm was well within an acceptable range of 60-100bpm. In all honesty I was feeling good health wise, I just needed to be wary of my back, every now and then I had a shooting pain through my right shoulder blade which could be excruciating, but as soon as it arrived it was gone leaving me to push on.

I sat at a table in the 'Illy' sponsored café (yes even at 4400m there are branded coffee houses), the benefits of globalisation and tourism eh, although this coffee house was waiting on its delivery and currently was unable to serve any coffee. I didn't mind, the breakfast tea was just as delicious. The whole far wall of the structure was a window with one of the most amazing views I had seen so far of the hills, snow-capped mountains and horses wandering about – it truly was a land of giants. I spotted a traveler coming towards the village up the same way we had come. First as a tiny dot in the distance then coming into form as a trekker with a huge pack slowly ambling towards the village. I now recognised the pace that the old man in Khumjung had suggested we adopt on all people, apart from children who seemed to have boundless energy, it was slow, steady and almost ponderous; to be honest the body can barely cope with more (there was definitely no running or yomping.) This traveler in particular had their head down, arms swinging lifelessly by their side with each foot touching down visibly heavily, from my experience the day before at this stage approaching Dingboche the smallest incline in the terrain made the muscles burn instantly with an overwhelming feeling of fatigue, as if you had been exercising for hours, and you probably had if you had followed the same stopping routine as Jun and I. Normally you don't feel these things walking these distance, but at this altitude sucking in air was far less rewarding, every movement mattered and so was measured by the required expense of effort and was considered for its necessity subconsciously – as I said, there was definitely no running.

It truly is an odd experience to be physically limited by this invisible force. I cannot overemphasise the need to acclimatise before heading up too high in altitude – I couldn't imagine the torture poor old Jun was experiencing. Although everyone experiences it differently, no one is completely impervious to AMS, unless you are Reinhold Messner who managed to climb Everest without supplemental oxygen and is quite literally a superhuman!

Sipping my tea, I watched a clique of women doing their washing outside in the surprisingly warm heat of the day; in the sun it was almost t-shirt temperatures. They had an ingenious invention for heating the water where a bowl of water was placed in what looked like a cradle on a reflective satellite dish, it appeared that the reflective surface heated the bowl or kettle. So simple and yet so effective especially when fuel and clean water were at a premium.

The women were laughing and joking, it was a constant surprise how everyone I had met so far in the Himalaya were so happy in the face of the obvious hardship and challenges of living in such a remote place. To be living 2 days walk, to the nearest 'town' in this day and age, for a westerner is just unfathomable. The weather can be full of extremes too, flitting between an intense heat in the day and sub-zero at night. The sun is also extremely intense at this altitude too due to the thin air less able to filter the harmful UV rays, evident from the leather like brown faces of the locals (mine was getting there too). And yet, despite these things the views and the environment seemed genuinely worth it, and the smiles and warm demeanour of the locals suggested this too. I fantasised more than once on my walk about a cabin in the mountains (and as I write this now, looking back, I still do!)

I tried to message Glaiza, but it failed, there was no network service and still no Wi-Fi, the feeling of isolation here is juxtaposed quite marvelously by the ridiculous notion that I was sat in a coffee shop reflecting on my journey so far, albeit without coffee but with one of the sweetest and most delicious cinnamon and apple pies I had ever had.

Nepal is a very lovely place. Nepali people do everything with a smile and have a good sense of humour. Every time I had crossed paths with someone or even made eye contact 'namaste' had been exchanged, literally meaning 'I greet the God that is in you'. Very polite. I was also impressed by the local's general levels of English. Okay, granted I was on one of the world's most popular trekking routes, but it was all people who showed proficiency, old, young, Sherpas or farmers, some who without being rude one would not have thought would have been able to speak any words let alone have a full and thorough conversation. It was great. The Sherpas were the best, carrying loads in excess of 20kg for hours on end, they were always happy to chat (though less so when under the formidable weight of their packs) sharing their stories of Everest and general advice for the trail. It was funny how I would often bump into the same Sherpas throughout the day as we all were headed roughly the same way. There was a real sense of camaraderie on the trail.

A Yak herder entered the village trailing behind a line of Yak that, quite uniformly walked up the path that split the village passing up and through the middle.

Yaks are amazing creatures, they can't survive below a certain elevation, but here dot the landscape like cows back home and are really very clever. They follow the leader who always seems to know the way to go and selects the best paths for their footing. The herder or shepherd follows behind. Whether snow, ice, stone or sand they always seem sure footed and as far as beasts go are quite attractive with their long shaggy coats. One important factor to note for a trekker is to stay mountainside as you meet them on the trail as the Yak always takes the easiest route which one doesn't want to mean bumping you off the side, however, though they are giant animals and look fierce they are in fact as docile as cattle, friendly even.

I spoke to the owner of the café, she told me they rent the shop as a business but themselves live in Kathmandu. She acknowledged that living this high up was hard being 4 days walk from Lukla, especially for her ageing mother. It was a good business to have but by the end of seasons she was often ready to get back to city life. She told me of farmers who preferred it up there and rarely left the mountains, I commend this, but the lifestyle must be very basic and quite solitary. She agreed explaining that this valley we were in was closed off to the outside world and trekkers between June and August because the government grows barley – extremely lonely for those living there. I did question this though, I couldn't understand why growing barley would mean the region had to be shut down? She too didn't know why.

I finished my tea and decided to go and get Jun to test his O2 level. My back was aching, and I was considering the 2-3-hour trek to Dughla ahead of me the next day, it would be difficult as was generally uphill by about 400m in quite a short space of time. I didn't think Jun was up to that. If I felt good which I hoped would, I intended to push on past Dughla to Lobuche 700m up as suggested by the Sherpas. I would make the decision in the morning based on my body, I had more than enough time to make the journey to EBC and back and thence my flight to KTM from Lukla. In my head I was thinking Dughla, Lobuche, Gorak Shep (EBC), Kala Patter, Dughla, Namche Bazaar, Lukla – 7 days maximum. Though I could be persuaded to stop in Tengboche again to see the monastery properly – that truly had been an amazing place.

As I got back to the guest house, Jun spoke first and told me he had already made his mind up to head down to Pangboche to see if this would help him acclimatise. It went without saying that I would continue on alone. In my head I knew that going down, even just to Pangboche would mean he wouldn't come back. I was quite sad to lose him in the end, although I had not intended to do this with a friend or partner and had planned it as a solo trek, he had been a great companion to while away the days and very quickly we had understood each other's patterns, 4 days had felt like 4 weeks. I prayed he would feel better as the night before he had quite literally been in tears which is a horrible thing to see. Saying goodbye was an emotional moment, and I hoped we would pass each other or at least be able to meet for a beer in Kathmandu. Sadly, this was not to be as Jun would return straight home once back in Kathmandu.

Next day I would be alone, I decided I would push for Lobuche and stop in Dughla for coffee. This would mean a 5 hour trek the next day but, all being well I would be only 1 day from EBC, I was so excited. I felt a little lonely without Jun as I turned to see him cresting the hill and not look back, so used to him I had become, I was now alone and without signal or Wi-Fi, I was missing my brother and girlfriends voice. I so much wanted to share what I was doing but currently only had my diary – for now it would do. I went to sleep dreaming and excited for the next leg of the journey, hoping that in Lobuche I would be able to send out a message to let everyone at home know I was okay.

Day 11 –Dingboche (4410m) - Lobuche (4910m)

8/3/2016

It was strange waking up without Jun, I was sure that for him he had made the best decision to go back, I couldn't help but feel disappointed though, as I imagined how I would have felt put in the same position.

Now on my own I was beholden to no one and so quickly rose from bed. Eager to get going, I packed my bag (redistributing the weight in light of how the bag had sat so uncomfortably on the way to Dingboche) and was ready to go by 7:00am. I removed a couple of small packs of muesli from my pack that I had bought in KTM that I hadn't got to eat, knowing that at this stage, based on my reduced appetite I wouldn't get near them. Although I was exercising all day, carrying a pack and trekking undulating terrain, I rarely felt hungry, it seemed the body just got tired, but rarely did I encounter an empty feeling one normally gets after sustained activity. I thought about stories I had read of people heading to the poles or those climbing mountains like Everest and literally wasting away due to the calorie deficit. They would talk of this inability to eat enough if any due to a combination of the nonstop exertion and elevation, both known appetite suppressors.

I said my goodbyes to people I knew I would be unlikely to see again, the Thai couple, Prichaya Suthivet and Pakawat Thongcharoen, were heading off in different direction heading towards the 3 passes trek and Chukhung village, this was an extension to the EBC trek that takes you, as it says, through three extremely high, and extremely cold mountain passes. At this stage in Dingboche if you have any AMS symptoms, do not even consider this as the route keeps you at a higher elevation for longer, the views are said to be worth it though.

As I left for Lobuche I headed north, the landscape being much like the day before, stone walls and half run down buildings that looked like old farmhouses. Now I had been told about the barley farming I knew that despite the decrepit appearance they were very much working buildings for the farmers and herders likely to house farmers overnights in the summer or store grain or barley at harvests.

I was making swift progress as the morning passed, with my iPod in I found myself in Dughla in no time – it had only been a 200m ascent and the walk had been very pleasant consisting of small, grassy hills heading steadily upwards. I had considered staying in Dughla to break the journey up and manage the elevation, but after good advice in Dingboche, and feeling very good and strong after a day's rest, I was convinced to push on the extra 300m or so. It is interesting how at this point I was no longer measuring distance or time, but rather in metres to ascend – as if this was the metric that held the highest import on both myself and my body.

At Dughla I enjoyed a very sweet milk tea and sat with a Chinese guy called Wang Cheng Long who was on holiday. I caught him sticking a Chinese flag on the wall, the lodge owner didn't mind as there were innumerable others from all over the place. On the trek it seemed that this is what a lot of the trekkers tended to do, a more sophisticated equivalent of 'I was here'. Wang had a stack of mini flags and stickers in his hand, as if everywhere he was going in Nepal is was going to leave his 'tag'. Jun had been the same by carrying a large Korean flag, his had been nicely pressed and protected in a sealed plastic bag – handled with such care and almost reverence. This must be what patriotism looks like, it's true that us 'Brits' no longer think like this, maybe a hangover or embarrassment from our Imperial history, or maybe just a sign of an evolving, multi-national, cosmopolitan nation. Doing something like they were doing had never even occurred to me.

I asked Wang how he was finding Nepal, he said he had been shocked, and not in a pleasant way. In the two weeks he had been in the country no one had spoken any Chinese apart from the specially sourced guide he had had. I myself wasn't surprised, in fact what did surprise me and always did was that he imagined that Nepali people would or should speak some Chinese – why would they? As I had this thought, I was reminded of travelling British and American tourists, who unquestionably expect (and mostly find) foreign nationals speaking our own mother tongue, the irony of my hypocrisy hit me over the head. I am sure as Chinese investment continues to flood into the Himalayan nation tourists like Wang Cheng Long will experience a different Nepal, as the country woos their financiers. In Asia, if not the world, there has been a shift in the balance of power, much like the moves over the last thousand years from Latin, to French and most recently to English, maybe the rest of the world will shift from English to Chinese?

After I finished my tea, I paid my bill and decided to push on to Lobuche. Supposedly this was meant to be a 2 ½ hour trek, I was however under no illusion that this one would be harder than the morning and would probably take longer if I allowed for rest stops.

Immediately the ascent began aggressively upwards with the path disappearing into an absolutely massive boulder field. Every step was exhausting, and I had to keep pausing for breath, a bit like the walk up to Namche Bazaar. Thank God I had audiobooks to take my mind off the strain (Big Finish – Doctor Who – God bless you!) After what felt like an eternity but was really no more than probably twenty minutes the route levelled out slightly, I sat down to guzzle some water and catch my breath. The Indian family I had seen several times joined me and sat down. The mother was in good shape and smiling, although she was adamant she would not be doing anything like this again, the young daughter was altitude sick and was not enjoying herself at all, in my opinion the trek would be a tough ask for a young teenager, I imagined the mother was having a rough time of it trying to keep her daughters spirits up.

Pushing on the way quickly got steeper again, I was having a hard time focusing on continuing when all I really wanted to do was rest, and the little voice inside me was encouraging me to do so, trying to justify to me why I should keep stopping for a break. Eager to get to the destination I fought it and pressed on. Again, the route flattened out onto a kind of plateau where there were many stone monuments and prayer flags dedicated to those that had lived and died on Everest and the trail, both Sherpas and climbers. This is clearly a holy place and to be honest, under the eternal watchful gaze of these Himalayan giants you feel it. It was quite an eerie spot, with nothing but the sounds of ruffled prayer flags blowing in the wind. A herd of yak crested the path behind me with their bells jangling breaking the quietude.

I was now at the edge of the Khumbu glacier that runs all the way to base camp. I was surprised that this part of the route was not easier, in my mind I had the impression that once the way leveled out there would be a well-trod path to follow. How wrong I was, the path had completely disappeared, and I was literally hopping over frozen streams and navigating around, over and through rock and boulder fields. At times I was even wondering if I had not in fact taken a wrong turn (this was and is almost impossible when you considered the direction, the lay of the mountains and the glacier). It was perhaps the first time I realised that yak poo was probably the best way to follow as they always take the easiest route, no doubt they were going the same way I was going, so follow the poo I thought.

My latest audiobook ended just as I spotted Lobuche (4910m) and my destination of the Eco Lodge. I was sure Jun would not have caught me up, I wasn't even sure he would have made it to Dingboche, let alone Dughla. I stopped a couple of walkers coming the other way and asked how they had found the final stretch, it seemed like my plan for base camp and Kala Pattar (EBC) was a good one.

I ordered a Sherpa stew which is a high energy food containing all sorts of bits and pieces. There were strips of what I wasn't sure was either fat or Chicken, as I couldn't tell and had heard scare stories about meat on the trail, I picked these bits out. I did not want to risk a bad stomach at this point so close to the end, I had been good sticking to the vegetarian options and had thus far suffered no ill side effects from the food.

I then charged my iPod, to make sure it was full for the next day's hike. It had really come into its own today proving invaluable taking my mind off in the more difficult periods. I tried to call Glaiza, but the poor signal and lack of Wi-Fi meant this was a no go. As I spoke about this to the lodge owner, he offered me to use his phone (of course I would have to pay). She didn't pick up initially but immediately called back and we finally spoke. It had been a long week without contact and I knew she would be worried, I had missed her a lot, just sharing the little day to day bits and hearing her voice. It is great to have these adventures, but it is almost as if unless you can share it with someone it isn't complete, I realised in this moment that although I can be quite a solitary person at times craving alone time and peace, at others I need contact and company, such a Gemini, never content.

Having spoken to Glaiza and letting her know I was okay I returned to my room to read and relax, excited as the next day, I was going to EBC!

Day 12 -

Lobuche (4910m) – Gorak Shep (5125m) – EBC (5364m)

9/3/2016

I was up by 6:00am but had to wait until nearly 7:00am to check out, I was a bit early for the owner which surprised me as usually on the trail someone always seemed to be up and about in the early hours, if not all the time. The day ahead was projected to be around 2-3 hours to Gorak Shep where I could get lunch before trying for EBC straight away. Very quickly I realised that heading out quickly without breakfast was foolish, as finally, on this last stretch I would be hampered by the altitude and the back that had given me increasing irritation would now make a full on assault on my senses. The rucksack had been fabulous on a few previous trips where I had backpacked between places, now though it was proving to be nothing but cumbersome and awkward. It was a large volume which made it ideal for short hops, however the sheer width and dimensions meant distributing the weight evenly was difficult causing several hot spots to appear on the back and aches on the shoulders and blades. It could be excruciating one minute before dissipating the next depending on how the weight was sat. Infuriating.

The route I was taking continued north again, and unlike the area around the glacier, this route seemed relatively clear and well-trod, I didn't need to think too much and followed subconsciously for a time enjoying the majestic views in front of me made up of the world's tallest mountain range. Without me realising the path disappeared, and I found myself in the midst of the Khumbu Glacier again. Logic told me I would have to skirt around again whilst heading in the same direction. The ground, being a mix of rock and sand with patches of ice made for slow progress. I resorted to my foolproof navigation method of following the yak poo again. It was a truly moon like landscape, and one in which at this early part of the day I seemed to be mostly walking on my own.

The way I was going, I realised I would have to cut across the Changri Glacier, the whole route was constantly changing with evidence of landfalls and the constant reverberations of tumbling rocks. My pace was slow as I picked my way through with only a compass point for direction.

As the morning passed on, more and more porters started coming towards me, bringing packs ahead of the trekkers that would be on their way back, presumably from base camp. This was a good sign and confirmed I was heading the right way, if I had been in any doubt before.

The sun rose higher in the sky and I had to unbutton my shirt as I was warming up with the exercise, the supposedly short two-hour trek from Lobuche was taking far longer than I wanted. My body was really struggling, the bouldering aspect of the walk, clambering up, across and around huge monolithic blocks meant naturally an increased heart rate and therefore obvious exertion, and this coupled with my already aching back meant I really felt I was having to push myself; There was a certain angle where each time I turned a certain way a barbed shooting pain shot across my neck and into my shoulder blade. This pain, whatever it was, would trouble me for a few months after my return from Nepal – though at the time it was all I could do to not to wince with the spasm. The journey's end was so close though, EBC, it was this thought that drove me that final bit. I didn't realise at the time, but this clamour over the rocks was in fact the final stage, the rocks were what was left of debris pulled down the hillsides as the glacier wound its way through the valley.

It was with genuine elation that from the top of a ridge I spotted the stage outpost that was the Gorak Shep camp. Apparently, this had been the location of the failed Swiss attempt to scale Everest in 1952. My journey from Lobuche was expected to have taken roughly 2 ½ hours, my stopwatch said it was nearer 4. My breakfast had now become my lunch and so after checking into the Buddha Guest House I quickly wondered how best to approach EBC, I wanted to leave straight away and wondered if there was anyone else. I spied a few faces I had met en route to Gorak Shep over the week who also had it in mind to make an assault straight away, so I would not be alone.

It was strange a strange feeling stood in the reception area seeing all the faces of people I recognised from the trail. We had all made our own way to Gorak Shep, but now, we found our destinies entwined as we all sought the same goal. A pair of Australian guys (Aaron and Christian) and a Chinese lady (Hua – who repeatedly emphasised she was American) were eating before heading out. I asked if they didn't mind if I too after refueling could join them, they didn't seem to mind, at least the guys didn't, Hua was a lot harder to read. In the short time I had been around them, she had more than once exclaimed how irritated she was to be part of a group as she had paid for a solo guide. For my part, we were all headed the same way, so it didn't really make a difference whether alone or part of a group at this stage on the trail.

After a quick lunch we all set off, excited but all visibly weary; we had all trekked up from Lobuche that same day, interesting as I hadn't passed some of them. There was no sense that everyone was in the mood for this last push for EBC, there felt like there was a cloud over the group as we walked in single file from the accommodation block. A combination of fatigue and people suffering at various degrees with AMS symptoms meant it appeared more of a chore. The energy sapping altitude was now making its presence fully known and the prospect of a 6 hour round trip was not necessarily one to look forward to, however in my mind the thought that in a little under 3 hours we would be stood at base camp, for me, gave me that little extra push I needed; I couldn't wait.

The first stage took us over a dry lakebed before heading back up into a mountain range at about 5000m skirting around the Khumbu Glacier. Every step was a trial, especially uphill and every downward step a reminder of the return leg that would be in not much more than a few hours. The glacier itself became the route as we made our way onto and across the huge mass of ice and rock. The temperature dropped perceptibly encouraging swifter movement, in spite of the burning lungs and muscles. The landscape was reminiscent of a desolate moonscape, a palette of greys, blacks and whites.

Milan, the groups Nepali guide stopped suddenly and waited for us to all catch up. He turned and pointed to 'Everest'. We stopped too. He informed us that this would be the best view we would have of the mountain on the whole march both to and from base camp. This surprised me, apparently at base camp you can't actually see the mountain very well, if at all. The black peak was currently poking out between a number of other 7000m+ peaks. No sooner had I got my camera out and taken a picture than the peak was obscured by fog and mist rolling in. Conditions change very quickly at this altitude so when you spot that perfect picture moment by the time you pull out your camera (which is mostly packed away so far inside a pack as you don't want to drain the battery in the cold) the moment usually passes.

I just found it hard to believe that from base camp we wouldn't be able to see Everest, this is something I, like many others just couldn't comprehend and was a disappointing reality, as I saw EBC as the end point. However, this is why so many climb Kala Pattar instead, not to get a lovely sunrise view of the mountain, but to get a lovely view at all! In fact, the only reason people want to get to base camp (which itself is not in an exactly fixed place due to rock falls and glacial movements) is the historical significance of the 'concept' of a base camp, as well as to feel the hum and buzz of activity if it is climbing season.

Continuing on, we came to an uphill section of path that ran on and for what felt like forever, before falling suddenly to a table of rock that sat perched like an island in the glacier, on one end of which stood a pile of pebbles, rocks and stones wrapped in prayer flags with a hand written sign saying 'Everest Base Camp.'

Northwards, a kilometre or so away from where we were I could see a small group of orange tents, this is what I took for the actual base camp for the climbers; we were at the semi-permanent tourist base camp, to keep us out of the way and also probably because of the dangers present of rock fall and avalanche as happened the year before in 2015. Being stood on an island in the middle of the glacier was probably far safer than being next to the mountainside where shifting snows and ice mean a continual risk of tumbling rock and avalanche.

At EBC there were about 20-30 of us all sharing that moment of elation, savouring the experience. Knowing that this feeling was temporary I was trying to capture every second. We all had our own reasons for wanting to go to base camp, be it the challenge, the stunning scenery or something much more personal. I knelt and said a prayer and buried Mum's picture a few feet from the pebble mound.

My story for heading to the Himalaya was after my Mum passed away in the latter part of the previous year. I saw the trip as an escape to reflect on what had been a very difficult period for our family. In fact, for Willy, my brother and I it had been a very difficult 5 years, from when Dad had also passed after a short illness. Mum had never been the same and had struggled daily from then.

In my mind, visiting Everest was a sort of pilgrimage, in some way by being near the highest point on earth it would act as a sort of conduit to the heavens where I could say goodbye in my own time, and in my own way, before returning back home, back to life, and back to a new beginning.

As I patted down the debris, sand and stone on the radiant picture of my Mum, a photo taken against a backdrop of flowers on a bright summer's day, I saw her smiling back at me, and in that instant felt her with me, I would hold that moment in my memory as long as I live. This journey to base camp had been about so many things but mostly, quite simply, about reconnecting with myself and cleansing the sadness so that all I would be left with were memories of joy and the better times. Not to forget the pain, but to better manage it.

A huge weight lifted from my shoulders as I stood and wiped a tear from my eye. 'I love you Mum' I thought, 'thank you.'

I stood looking at our Earths highest mountain range and felt immense pride. Just drinking it in.

The one thing all of us shared, if not our purpose was the achievement, we were from all nations and all ages, but we had all chosen this journey. During the build up to the trek people I had spoken to were divided into two camps, some people couldn't see the difference between a 14-day hike/trek and actually climbing the mountain, they considered it almost the same thing; it isn't. Although hard work and exhausting at altitude the only real danger was the ever prevalent AMS and staying on the somewhat precarious cliff hugging trails. Others knew someone who had done the trip to EBC and suggested it was a lot easier than was made out and would be little more than a tramp across the Brecon Beacons; again, it isn't. It is certainly no hike up Pen y Fan and does require some semblance of conditioning as the terrain is uneven and mostly uphill. However, if you are cautious with the altitude and do some physical preparation like staying on your feet for long periods of time it is achievable for most people. I had made it harder on myself by carrying my own bag and probably going quicker than the usual tours.

It had been so interesting at the end of each day to share experiences of Nepal and the trek in the lodges and was surprising how differently people were experiencing it. For me, the trek *had* been more of a physical challenge as each day I had to shove my pack on and set off uphill for 10km+. I had spent many of my days with porters discussing breathing strategies, breaking strategies, hydration, packing strategies and simple methods of carrying the pack on the back to best spread the loads economically. Hearing people complain in the evenings of tiredness, aching feet and sore backs when they had been shepherded by a guide following their packs that had set off hours before them to be at their base for that day always made me smile. I myself had chosen a more physical challenge to push myself and felt satisfied that I had chosen my way, it had felt all the more real than if I had done it differently. That is not to say that my way is the best way and that my achievement surpasses those others, to pardon the phrase, we all have our own Everest's to climb.

I partook in the back slapping and high fives with the strangers all around as we shared this wonderful feeling and moment at the camp, knowing that it would be all too brief and before long we were on our way back. By this point I was now suffering AMS symptoms, nothing compared to Jun, but a headache and sore throat were now an ever present. My peak was between 4900-5300m, I think to go above that would have required a bit more time to acclimatise, possibly at Dingboche. As it was, I was already on the return leg so hopefully wouldn't suffer for long.

Once back I could see I wasn't alone in my suffering. I managed to force some food down although I was far from hungry (a Nepali style mushroom pizza) and armed with 2 litres of water I took myself off to bed at 6:00pm. I would be up early around 4:00am for Kala Pattar so thought it best to get some rest especially in light of the fatigue I was feeling. I was surprised that no one else was celebrating with a beer after reaching base camp, then again, with the thought that most would be getting up early like myself it probably wasn't the best idea. Also, alcohol at this stop was quite expensive (around 500-600 rupees) as well as the fact that alcohol dehydrates which, when we were already dehydrating faster with the altitude and exertion meant no one hung about for a celebration and all sloped off early.

Fully clothed I tucked myself into my sleeping bag feeling quite cosy, yet sleep was hard to come by, in fact it was all in all a horrendous night. My pre-trip reading had told me that at altitude most people have restless sleep, I could vouch for this as each day I had crept higher my nights rest had become more and more broken. It was with both frustration and relief that my watch displayed 4:00am. I went to take a swig of my water which had frozen, it appeared this morning would be a cold one, -8 Celsius as we set off, though with the wind chill it felt much colder – we would have to move fast to keep warm and wake up.

Day 13 - Gorak Shep (5125m) – Kala Pattar (5540m) – Pheriche (4240m)

10/3/2016

I fought the urge to stay wrapped in the haven of my sleeping bag, but knew it was pointless, I could hear movement in the hallway as others were getting up to head out. For a brief second I thought 'is it worth it?' thinking I would rest a bit longer, but as soon as the thought presented itself, I knew I was doing the typical and making excuses, this forced me up immediately.

I blew my nose and 'hocked' my throat, it is disgusting to be sure but at 5000m+ the amount of mucus clinging to my throat was not very pleasant, like syrup sticking to a plate. As I stood looking out the window at the deep impenetrable blackness we would be heading out into my head throbbed with every beat of my heart, I was not looking forward to the exertion, the destination definitely, the journey not so much. Gorak Shep is not at a natural elevation for living, although the early part of the EBC trek had allowed me to largely become accustomed to elevations over 4000m, once you hit 5000m, no one is immune to nature.

We set off, and by we, I mean pretty much the same group who went to EBC the day before, at about 4:30am; all with head lamps. The aim was to crest the peak of Kala Pattar at 5540m around 6:30am to see the sun rise and glimpse the majestic beauty of the Himalayan range, with a rainbow of colours reflecting off the peaks. I was especially excited to see the Queen of them all properly, clearly, and close - Chomolungma, Sagarmatha, Everest. (side note, it always makes me chuckle that a mountain in both Tibetan and Nepali is considered a female Deity, Mother Goddess of the Universe and Goddess of the Sky respectively but is named in English after a Welsh male surveyor – George).

What occurred over the ensuing 2 ½ hours I cannot describe, the biting coldness and the feeling of complete and utter exhaustion was something I was quite unaccustomed to and almost overwhelmed me, I was genuinely fed up. It was only with sheer will I struggled on knowing that it was my head trying to get me to choose the more comfortable option of going back. We scrambled up a dirt track that in the lack of light was quite frightening at times and summited numerous 'false peaks' only to realise that the path continued zig zagging upwards. As the sun rose the astounding scenery helped drive me on – the views were incredible, and getting better with every few steps

There was also more than a hint of competitiveness between the group that pushed us all as we verbally nudged each other when one seemed to be struggling, most of the way someone seemed to be openly moaning serving only to spur the group on not wanting to be the one holding everyone else up. To contemplate quitting at this point, for me was inconceivable, some of the others needed more encouragement as more than once Hua sat on a rock tearfully stating she couldn't go any further. Deep down I knew no one wanted to quit.

Kala Pattar is 300m higher than EBC, and it felt it. For some reason, maybe because we hadn't yet acclimatised to this elevation it seemed far higher and the journey seemed to take far longer, though in reality it was only two or so hours before we finally reached the highest point, a stone mound that divided the 'peak' from the piles of rubble surrounded by the typical prayer flags and a not so surprising number of other people milling about for the sunrise.

My hands and feet were absolutely frozen and with the thumping headache I had endured pretty much since arriving at Gorak Shep, I found it hard to focus and enjoy the amazing sights in front of me, all I could think of was I hope the sun rises quickly as I was freezing and wanted to get moving straight away. With these thoughts on repeat the sun did begin to rise, again Everest was mostly hidden apart from the peak, the black fish tail jutting out between the top of two equally massive, but less tall mountains. As I stood rocking on a stone looking at the multi-hued oranges, yellows and reds reflecting off the magical mountains I began to realise that without this single moment, stood freezing with a literally blinding headache at 6:30am on Kala Pattar watching the sunrise, the Everest trip might have been more than a little disappointing, as this was mostly what I came to see and without visiting Kala Pattar, you may not even have had a proper glimpse apart from the snatched view on the trek to EBC, to visit Base Camp was really just for the sense of achievement. If I could give anyone some advice it would be don't consider this side trek optional, make Kala Patter an essential part of your journey, spend the extra day or night to ensure you see the sunrise, that incredible moment, and it is literally just a moment, when the sun hits the peak emitting a shower of colour that radiates the morning sky, it is a moment that will live with me forever and was what I had thought of and indeed hoped Base Camp would have provided. Kala Pattar was my Base Camp.

I took some spectacular pictures of Everest as we made our way back at 9:30am for breakfast and then to check out. There was little time to really savour the experience as no one wants to hang around and linger at that altitude, though without the headache it would have been an amazing place to stay a few days and to just enjoy 'being'.

On reflection, Kala Pattar had been one of the toughest things I had ever done, indeed the EBC trek had been a real challenge, carrying the weight and adjusting to the altitude had been more difficult than I had anticipated, despite my reading and research beforehand, the effect on the individual is really something you can't prepare for until you are there in the thick of it.

Once I checked out, I made my return to Lobuche along the trail back on my own. I reflected on my experience the last few days and in fact over my time in Nepal, I felt different, changed. It really felt like I had finished something, like the end of a chapter, in more ways than one.

I planned to stay at Pheriche which was 4240m – almost 1000m below where I had stayed the day before which I was sure would help my minor AMS. Pheriche was the other side of the hill to Dingboche and 200m lower via a walk down an adjacent valley to the one I had come up following the Lobuche Kola.

In Dughla as I sat with a coffee, I met a young Swiss guy who seemed unconcerned with altitude and was intending to do Kala Pattar and EBC in one day – 'good luck mate!' I thought. Then again, he is probably more at home being from near the Alps than I was. I would have been interested to have known how he would get on.

There was no distinct path as I made my way down from Dughla, but I could see Pheriche in the distance and so made my way as easy as I could across fields and what I assumed were farms. I bumped into a pair of porters that I had met earlier on the trail so knew I was on the right path.

In the fields leading up to Pheriche I saw many tents again for a company that was doing excursions to Everest, I assume these were companies offering ascents.

I decided to stay in the Himalayan lodge where I met two Americans, one seemed quite ill with AMS, they had yet to get to base camp, looking at one of them I didn't think he would make it.

My friends from Gorak Shep joined us later in the afternoon, I had been eager to get here so had not hung around. Hua seemed to come alive in the two Americans presence wanting to talk all things American, maybe it was the decreasing altitude or maybe it was the fact she was in the company of countrymen that made her so different, so animated, so verbose; I had never recovered our relationship from when I had asked if she was Chinese, 'I was born there but I'm an American'. I could see the Aussie guys with her were tired of her company, looking and hearing her now I could see how a week together could wear on you, so they quickly made their excuses after a small dinner to move away to a different part of the room.

In the centre of the room sat a large oven which is quite common in the public/dining rooms in the lodges. When lit, the warmth acts as a kind central heating and meeting point. I took my boots off to warm my feet, the Australian pair joined me and we all just sat in silence, the American guys also joined us before long leaving Hua to finish her food.

At about 7:00pm I called it a day, knowing that the next day I would be heading to Namche Bazaar, a journey that on the ascent is usually split into two days due to elevation and incline, so would take me in the region of 7 hours. Now that I had been to Base Camp and seen the sunrise at Everest, I now had the mentality that I just wanted to get going, back to Lukla, back to Kathmandu, back down to my next adventure.

Day 14 - Pheriche (4240m) – Namche Bazaar (3440m)

11/3/2016

I wanted to get off early, so after a quick coffee, Spanish omelette (really only potato) and a chat about my bag with some porters who questioned the weight (even they thought it was a little on the heavy side for a foreigner) I made my way at 7:30am, it was going to be a long day.

I said goodbye to the group who I had shared some amazing moments with, agreeing to meet them for a beer at Namche Bazaar but even as I said it inside I wasn't sure I really meant it, I think they thought the same and together we did the charade of see you soon knowing this was probably goodbye for good. Setting off my back felt okay although a slight twinge in my shoulder blades.

Very quickly I was crossing the small footbridge to that took me towards Dingboche on the way up, I was now literally retracing my steps all the way to Lukla. It was amazing how parts of the journey looked new; I couldn't remember some of the scenery as if seeing for the first time.

I adjusted the straps on my bag, and this seemed to take all the pain away, if the aches had been from poor positioning on my back and something I could have wholly managed this was poor admin on my part and definitely a lesson learned. I was quickly reminded the pain wasn't fully gone, better, but not eradicated. With my headphones in and Bernice Summerfield audio plays, (a Doctor Who spin-off character and audios from the superb Big Finish range –

highly recommended.) I was flying through Pangboche and the like in no time.

After a long uphill slog and about 2 1/2 hours I entered Tengboche. The famous EBC trail bakery was closed and when I went into the lodge I had stayed at, it was empty, much less the coke I wanted being available, and I was told that there wasn't even tea or coffee. Disappointed and a little frustrated, I decided to use the toilet and sort out what were increasingly cracked lips with some balm. When I returned to my bag in the main lodge room, I was spotted by the lodge owner who recognised me from my stay a couple days previously. It seemed they had been cleaned out by a couple of groups (I must have missed them somehow, they must have gone the Dingboche way) but she did have water, which I bought gratefully, and a chocolate bar. The owner also updated me with regards to Jun. It turned out he had not gone down to Pangboche as we had discussed but had in fact come all the way back to Tengboche where she had given him an internet card for his phone, and then he had continued on to Namche. I can only imagine that he had descended and had started to feel better and so continued further and further to the point that coming back was not an option for him. So, he had given up after all. I was so sad for him, although this is what I thought he probably should do after the way the AMS had taken him, it was still sad to know that he had not achieved his goal. Later I would have a Facebook message from him telling me he had just felt too ill and that he was then in Kathmandu but heading home immediately – I wouldn't see him again.

From Tengboche there had been that horrible uphill section that had seemed to carry on forever, which had now become a painful downhill as my sweaty feet were slipping and therefore rubbing against my boots and pressing against the fronts, maybe my nails were too long I wondered. It also felt much warmer than the day we had come up, as what had been slight snow that day had given way to blazing sunshine. When I reached the valley floor and after crossing the wide steel bridge with the café at one end, there was again a long uphill stretch.

After about 5 hours on my feet I stopped for lunch at a place with a fabulous view of the valley itself, surrounded by mountains. The place was grossly overpriced, no doubt due to the view but was so worth it. The owner made sure my rice had no garlic and went on to tell me that her husband had been Prince Charles' personal guide 30 years previously and that they had even been invited by him a few years ago to the Palace for tea - amazing! I was so tired at this point so struggled to keep the conversation going, I think this lovely lady was disappointed, as an anglophile to meet a Brit was opportune, sadly this Brit offered such poor company, and for her part her stories were some pretty big guns to bring to the table!

The final part of walk took me along via the Chorkung Ridge, I wandered in a bruised but fantastic haze of adrenaline, excitement and fatigue. My toes and back were sore but the views were incomparable as well as the feeling of achievement and pure appreciation of where I was.

I rocked up to the lodge at 2:30pm, about 7 hours after departing Pheriche. I washed and changed – again into dirty clothes as that was all I had and had a beer with dhal baat whilst finally managing to contact the family. A short but sweet notification, but it was a relief to let them know I was safe and that I had made it. At 6:00pm I headed up to a deep satisfied sleep knowing that the next day would mean another 5 hour or so trek on bruised feet with a sore back to Lukla, it didn't matter as I had been to EBC, was still high from the experience. The Himalaya truly are one of the most incredible places on earth and I felt and feel privileged to have spent 10 days amongst them.

Day 15 – Namche Bazaar (3440m) -Lukla (2860m)

12/3/16

It's funny, as I sat writing I was already back in KTM in a Lavazza coffee shop, though half the wares were unpurchaseable due to the load shedding. On the other side of a window from where I sat, I could see two monks with mobile phones in a quite classy bar drinking tea. Not really my view of denouncing the material world in search of enlightenment and nirvana – maybe what it means to be a modern monk has changed.

Anyway, back to the journey

Safe to say, my 5-hour expectation for making it back to Lukla was ambitious, it was, in the end, 7 1/2 hours of pain. It was as if all of a sudden, the switch in my body had gone and I was feeling aches and niggles everywhere. Sure, I was combining what had been my day 1 and day 2 to get back to Lukla, but it was mostly downhill. I had never envisaged it being such a mammoth finale, in my head it was planned as a nice stroll through the beautiful scenery – the reality was that my back was shot to pieces and my feet were battered, bloodied, blistered and bruised. The only saving grace was that after talking to others back in Lukla it seemed 90% agreed with me and had felt similar things on the way back from EBC, the other 10% were liars.

Thinking I only had 5 hours to the finish line I set off a little bit later than I normally would at around 8:30am. My body was tired, and it was only the fact that this was the last day that gave me the energy to throw the backpack on and put my boots on with my smelly wet socks. The 15kg of my pack today also felt a lot heavier

Walking away from Namche I looked back to have a final glance, it really is a marvelous and magical place. Sat in a valley surrounded by such enormous snow-capped mountains, a flight and couple of days walk away from the nearest city, Namche Bazaar in some ways was like stepping back in time; I could imagine the hubbub of explorers and climbers making their way to Base Camp and beyond and all the stories they would tell of their exploits in the mountains – I doubt I will see it again.

I checked into the TIMS outpost where the guard smiled and wrote 'out' on my card. I would have two more checkpoints to go through. He tried to sell me a certificate of completion (little entrepreneur.) As I stood there, I could feel shooting pains up my back again, I had the sense it was going to be a long day in more ways than one and really wanted to get on. The flood of emotion I had felt on departing Namche Bazaar faded fast as I made my long, slow, dusty, mule filled descent to the valley floor and crossed what must be the world's longest suspension bridge across the junction of the Bhote and Dudh Koshi rivers.

I am probably not being truthful when I suggest that I had forgotten the journey up to Namche Bazaar and how particularly arduous the final section had felt. I remember mentioning to Jun that I thought the section would be 'bugger' to go down; dry and dusty and pitted with stones to only assist any slippage as well as the innumerable twists and turns. It was punishing on the back, and with the weight of the bag the pressure on the knees was starting to show as they now felt tender and were visibly swollen. The continual interruptions of mules and yak trains only compounded the misery as they passed close enough to rub against me, I would start sneezing and my eyes would water – I'm allergic to horses and I guess the Equus genus in general to some extent.

After about 2 1/2 hours I entered Jorsale and the Sagarmartha entrance to checkout with my TIMS. I stood queuing for the next stamp on my card surrounded by a variety of tour groups wanting to come the other way. Not two weeks earlier I had stood there in the courtyard, on a lovely warm day with Jun, with not a tour group in sight. It was a reminder that I had just snuck into the back end of the off season and the reality that this was a major tourist trek, in a small way my bubble of isolation was burst as I was, from this point on, no longer going to be alone. It was strange, there had been times on the trip after I had left Jun where I had been a little lonely and wanted to chat, but now I knew that this period of isolation was over and that I would likely pass people every few minutes coming the other way I knew I would miss it. Some people are never satisfied I thought chastising myself. The season was beginning.

I managed to jump the queue as I caught the eye of the swamped worker, again this guy too wrote 'out' and gave me a knowing smile. I felt good.

The next stop, Mondjo, was not far as that had been where we had stayed the first night, my memory of the first day to Mondjo had been quite pleasant so I imagined the day to follow suit, how wrong I was. It seemed to take an age to make the next notable stop in Bengkar, I was so tired I stopped and bought a high sugar mango juice and mars chocolate bar. After a brief rest the sugar rush seemed to hit, and I felt ready to move off. I saw a sign stating that this was the half-way point to Lukla – I had been walking about 4 hours.

From Bengkar to Phakding the road seemed to be a never-ending wave of ups and downs from stone steps to dirt mounds in generally poor repair; signs of landslides were everywhere. Fortunately for me it was not the rainy season, evidence of the devastation it could leave behind was clear to see and obvious the challenge the locals face keeping the route safe, usable and clear. How did I miss so much on the way up?

I don't think the journey was actually taking that long but in my mind every second seemed like an hour. If I had been fresh I probably would just relaxed and enjoyed the stunning scenery it seemed like I was seeing for the first time, however with fatigue and the sore back it was as if time had stopped, every inch I was thinking about it, feeling it, measuring it, every step was an eternity, impossible to think of anything else.

Entering Phakding my pace had again tailed off too, now little more than a saunter. I had now been walking about 5 hours and it was touching 1:30pm. I ordered some lunch and asked how long to Lukla, apparently, I was still at least 3 hours away.

I finished my vegetable sandwich, fries and Fanta at the same place that I had met the Thai couple two weeks before and set off on what I was telling myself was the final stretch. I had seen through the window some of the others pass, those that I trekked to base camp with (an Australian man and his daughter) who were now up ahead with their porters.

I caught up with them around Ghat where they had stopped for some lunch, they too seemed to be feeling the heat which made me feel somewhat better.

Quickly moving on, it was no time before I caught up with a porter hidden under a massive pack. It is sad that I did not catch his name, as from day 2 we had walked with and past each other again and again and had stayed largely at the same lodges. Saying hi and namaste politely but with little actual conversation, now was a chance to rectify it.

We walked together chatting away. I was thirsty and so we stopped at a small local shop where I bought him a bottle of water. His English was excellent and he referred to me as the UK Sherpa as I was the only person he had seen recently carrying so much and so fast, I took this compliment with pride as I hadn't felt all that strong or quick – then again maybe this is why my body was so tired! My Nepali friend, as I will remember him, told me that he wasn't actually a porter but was a tour guide. Due to the low season he needed work, and despite portering paying only 200R per day, which compared to a guide's fee was extremely low, he needed to keep busy to provide for his family. To give an indication, the bottle of water I just bought him was 200R. He and his wife were 24 years of age. He invited me to meet his wife in Lukla, this was where we had intended to swap details, sadly this didn't happen as one of his colleagues on the trail had fallen back and was calling on him to wait.

Whilst talking he had told me how he was of the Rai caste that were native of this region and parts of India and that he was a Hindu. Although he qualified this by saying that he didn't really believe in God, just people. I am not sure if this was an idea or expression lost in translation, but it was a lovely sentiment. Previously he had worked in Malaysia but the money had not been great so he had returned home – hoping the coming season would be a busy one. His actual house was a further 2 days walk from Lukla, but he and his wife had wanted more and so realised they needed to move to the nearest big town – Lukla (note, Lukla is not a big town.) He had also been educated at the Hillary School of Khumjung which is probably why his English was so good. Hillary has had such a profound impact on this region and the people of Nepal – incredible.

Leaving my nameless friend just outside of Lukla just before the steep ascent to the gateway was a good way to end my trip, as it had begun, on my own with my own thoughts. I climbed the pebbled path as the odd smattering of people came the other way, I must have looked a sweaty mess. I had done it, I stood just inside the gateway and turned looking behind at the journey I had just been on, even now all those months later I cannot put into words fully the impact this place has had on me.

7 ½ hours after setting off I slumped down on a waist high wall feeling thoroughly proud. This had been the experience of a lifetime, everything I had wanted and more. I checked out finally at the last (or first) TIMS office and made my way back to the Lama lodge where I enjoyed a beer and lovely homemade BBQ chicken pizza – extravagant no doubt but well earnt! I had managed to rearrange my flight with the local Tara/Yeti airlines attendant for the next day. A 6:30am start beckoned which had now become the norm, I would be more than ready. Speaking to the attendant he suggested I would be the last person on the flight, and importantly that I would have to be the last to check in. I had no idea what he meant, maybe it was a weight issue? i.e. if the plane was running heavy, I would be bumped? In any case I trusted he knew what he meant and made my way

back to the lodge to rest. My last night in the Himalayas proper was peaceful satisfied one.

Day 16 - Lukla (2860m) - Kathmandu

13/3/2016

I woke very early, eager to get going and not miss my flight. I paid the lodge and the owners mum came and presented me with a khata, a white silk scarf to wish me a safe journey. Milan, the guide who I had walked with on and off over the past week said at the airport when we passed, that I must have been a good customer – an 800R pizza and 450R Tuborg beer would have helped no doubt.

The day before at the ticket office I had been handed what I thought was a new ticket, however, they had in fact only just written 7:00am on the departure time, no wonder I was told I had to board the plane last. As 7:00am approached I was getting anxious. Finally, the attendant from the previous day came and said hi pulling me to some rather large scales and ushered me to join the rest of the passengers. It was so chaotic but in a weird way it seemed to be working. Once I was sure that I had made it onto the passenger manifest (if indeed they even had one) I went and got myself a coffee and waited.

It was not until 9:30am that we lifted off from the worlds shortest and most dangerous runway surrounded by the Himalayas. It was extremely cloudy, so the view was not as spectacular as the outbound flight. We did hit a patch of turbulence, I say turbulence, but this was so violent the word hardly does it justice. It was a reminder of how small the tin machine was and indeed why this flight lane had one of the worst safety records in the world. I pulled my rosary out which made me feel a little better. Before long we landed, and I was in the back of a taxi driving through the polluted streets of Kathmandu headed towards Thamel, my accommodation and hopefully a hot shower.

Checking in the manager was surprised to see me so soon. As we chatted, he passed me an unpaid bill for momo (dumplings.) He smiled; he knew I would be back. He was worried as the room I had had was no longer available, so he showed me another room, though it was smaller than my previous one and he didn't think I would find it suitable – I really didn't care and to be honest, I thought it looked much more comfortable and fresher than the previous one.

Stepping under the hot shower after two weeks was an amazing feeling, I could see the brown water running off my body. The travel wash I had was not sufficient for my matted and greasy hair, so after a quick power nap I headed out to a shop for some real shampoo, body wash and of course – chocolate. I also managed to grab a cold beer and a coffee. This day was a bit of a write off, I was waiting for an update regarding my Bhutan trip and in preparation sent my clothes out to be washed. Tomorrow I would do some sightseeing again feeling almost clean, much more myself and human.

Day 17 – Kathmandu

14/3/2016

I woke about 5:00 am to see the load shedding had finished so put my bits on charge and went back to sleep before finally rising at 8:00am. I had been resting for 12 hours or so and still felt like I could rest some more, but I didn't want to waste my day so decided to head to Patan – a southern district of Kathmandu.

Patan had been a separate kingdom until invaded by the King of Kathmandu in 1768. The main attraction was their own Durbar Square, which was in all aspects the same as its Kathmandu counterpart, albeit on somewhat smaller scale and much less busy. I would walk off the tiredness I thought as the journey would only take about an hour and a half and would give an opportunity to see the south side of the city that I had yet to go to.

En route I stopped at Dalai La, a Tibetan themed boutique hotel. It was amazing to think that in Namche Bazaar I thought nothing of paying 750R for a big breakfast each day, yet here in the heart of Nepal and its capital city I almost baulked at the 600R price, I am glad I didn't though – it was a delicious omelette. Afterwards I enquired about room availability thinking maybe I would treat myself when I came back from Bhutan, I think they looked at my unkempt scruffy and unshaven appearance, dressed in a t-shirt and shorts and decided I was not the type of clientele they were looking for. Apparently, they were completely fully booked – including the suites. I checked online and that is not the impression I got.

I set off directly south through Thamel to get to Patan and was reminded of the stuffy cold I had had the first few days in Nepal, the pollution was horrendous, ancient diesel engines, dust tracks instead of tarmac and general grime fill the air and in most parts the sky is a muggy grey. I would imagine respiratory illnesses must be one of the top reasons for death in the city, the air was a complete contrast to the Himalayas.

Crossing the Bagmati river that delineated the cities southern section I was shocked, there was literal sewage flowing into it at a touching distance for walkers by. In a country that prides itself on the god given gift of natural beauty, they treat their 'holy' rivers like this, like latrines – and as if to add insult to injury as I was looking a woman threw a wrapper of some sort into the 'river'/sludge. So sad.

Walking the numerous main roads was like taking my life into my hands. At each junction police officers stood 'directing' traffic; I use this term loosely as blowing whistles and waving their hands around maniacally only seemed to contribute to the chaos more than anything else. I settled into groups of people shuffling across slowly, as if crossing in numbers was safer, like a waddle of penguins.

After a while the traffic thinned and the pollution lightened, blue sky peeking out of the gloom. I approached a white archway that served as the official entrance to Patan. For 500R I was given a pass to wear around my neck marking me out as a paying tourist and given a map. The neck tickets are an interesting way to try and get regular income, I was intrigued to see how they might enforce them if you wandered in by mistake as although I had headed directly for the arch, it was possible to circum-navigate the supposed entrance and enter a different way.

Walking around proved to be a real eye opener, the earthquake damage was far worse than anything I seen previously; it was literally everywhere, mounds of rubble dotted about and cracks tearing through the fabric of most buildings that were now only still standing because of being propped up by bamboo struts wedged at all angles. People didn't seem to notice nor acknowledge the devastation, continuing to live in and around the crumbling structures as if it was just a part of life. There were little to no signs of clearing away debris or rebuilding. I wonder whether the ticket money was contributing, in my heart, as with Kathmandu's Durbar Square, I knew likely not.

The square itself although smaller to the one in Kathmandu proper, was no less impressive – there were less people touting for guide work which meant wandering about was a much more pleasant experience. Having said that, no sooner had I let my guard down I was literally grabbed and manhandled by a museum worker ushering me towards a large reddish building. It seemed I was one of few tourists milling about that day, so he was doing his bit to drum up business. I didn't mind as I had read that the Palace museum was worth a visit so readily paid 400R to enter and access the other sections that were cut off from the main square and only accessible through the museum.

Entering, I quickly understood why the workers were so vigorously pulling in customers, clearly load shedding does not discriminate – there was no power with the only light being ambient and that which came through several tiny windows. I just couldn't understand so many things, but mostly how can you have a new museum in a reconstructed building (with the help of generous funds from Austria), light limited due to flawed design and lack of electricity because of load shedding making it unseeable, in the middle of the day. I couldn't make out half of the exhibits or the written descriptions. This was a crying shame as the bits I could make out were a basic introduction to the main tenets of Buddhism, Hinduism and the unique Nepali architecture. It was still fascinating but hard work causing eye strain. As it was it was interesting, but if I had been properly able to indulge myself it could have been a great museum (for example I learned how the Nepalese discovered a way to make their unique roofs with the long overhangs stay up, they use a thing called a 'tudal' that acts like a strut jutting out about 45 degrees – fascinating).

Despite the lighting issue I thoroughly enjoyed the museum and took some pictures where I could, but as I left, I just couldn't get my head around it, why not just get a generator like larger restaurants? This museum was meant to be the best in Nepal, which I could easily believe, why not do more to make sure it stands as an example for the best the country can provide? Why not go that extra mile to ensure that this bastion of Nepali culture and history is always available for the masses, not only for education, but even to just generate income? Then again, like so many aspects of Nepal, it is beyond my comprehension.

On my way back I stopped for a beer and walked via a temple called the Golden Temple monastery, this is where normal people live like monks – part time monks.

As I walked around, I was weighing up in my head how best to spend the remainder of my time in Nepal. I was still very tired from the trek to EBC and apart from heading to Bhutan, had a few days left to do something and didn't know whether to take another road trip to either Pokhara or

Lumbini (the birthplace of the Gautama Buddha) or just chill. The way I was feeling right now, wandering the streets of Kathmandu and reading sounded ideal.

Day 18 - Kathmandu

15/3/2016

Had an absolute result last night, for some reason I remembered that I had a VPN on my iPad. I managed to watch some TV which was a nice escape before bed. Willy my brother had been telling me about some Marvel TV shows on Sky so thought I might check them out.

I woke about 8:00am but lounged around until 10:00am – the shower was freezing, just as I was admitting defeat a lukewarm trickle replaced the ice-cold water. I decided I would go for a walk across town to some Hindu temples on the northeastern edge of town. I wasn't sure what to expect, having had very little experience with Hinduism, but was very intrigued as to what I would see. The walk itself was about an hour-ish, my feet were still blistered which made it a little painful and with coupled with some the heavy pollution meant walking was not as pleasant as I had hoped it might have been, although it was nice to wander and allowed for some thinking time. A few things crossed my mind as I thought about the trek and Nepal itself: -

Holding Hands – here men very comfortably cuddle, hold hands and walk thusly, very closely and seemingly intimately. It looked strange to me with my British eyes and sensibilities, it was just so unusual where in the UK even couples might refrain from such public displays of affection. There did not seem to be any sexual connotation in Nepal but just a sign of familiarity, kinship or close friendship. I was also struck by the fact that both men and women seemed to have little distinction with respect to their gender, Sherpas of both sexes tended to carry similar weights, and it was not unusual to see on building sites that they worked side by side doing the same kind of lifting. More than once I would also see a woman stomping around giving a man a verbal (and in some case physical) dressing down. And yet, Nepal, much like its close neighbour India, has a well-documented problem with both sexual and domestic violence against women – an obvious contradiction that was hard to reconcile based on what I was seeing.

Fast food – this is one of few times, the only other maybe being Ghana, that I had been to a place where there were only a handful, if any fast food restaurants. There were some quite funny 'alternative' substitutes much like the Starbucks in Lukla. I had also seen two empty KFCs in Thamel and a couple of recently closed Baskin Robins, but no McDonald's or actual Starbucks. It was refreshing to think about local restaurants and foods as options as opposed to defaulting to the typical global offerings. This led me to think of a quick way to enter the fast food market in Nepal – Momo. They were a local delicacy, much like Chinese dumplings. Yet there were no street vendors selling them and in restaurants they seemed to take ages to prepare and cook. If someone could, like in China, have stacks of steaming trays on say the back of a bike one might be able to make a quick buck.

Load Shedding – traffic lights are a real problem, now I see why there are so many traffic police diverting the flow of man, beast and machine. As you would expect there are loads of lights at junctions, but most are out of gas. You would think the government would ensure that key infrastructure would be exempt from the load shedding? Apparently not. Madness.

After an hour or so I eventually came towards Pashupatinath, a sacred Hindu temple complex that is located on the banks of the Bagmati River, immediately, as with everywhere in the city I could see evidence of the Earthquake. Some temples had been boarded off and others had quite literally crumbled to the ground. I bought my ticket to enter the area, a not so cheap 1000R which didn't include entrance to the main temple, just the grounds. Soon after getting my ticket I was joined by a guy who fell in step as I wandered along. We talked freely and his English was superb, he was clearly a guide but we didn't discuss this until the end of a semi walking tour of the area where I ended up giving 1000R, it should have only been around 500R, but after he, Krishnapur, showed me pictures of his family (2 daughters) and his home that had been devastated by the earthquake I couldn't help but want to give more. His family now lived under a blue tarpaulin on a cleared area right next to the pile of bricks that had once been his family home. Absolutely heart breaking to hear about and see, my experiences in Kathmandu so far told me that this wasn't just a line either as it seemed a large portion of the population were suffering similarly. Krishnapur also told me he had been part of Michael Palin's group of guides when he had visited for the 'Himalaya' documentary series. I really liked the guy and by name dropping Mr. Palin he had really pressed the right buttons with me.

Krishnapur had been excellent value, explaining about the gods depicted on the facades of the buildings, showing me friezes of the karma Sutra, and even where he had once met Mother Teresa (he was seriously name dropping my heroes –

I was just waiting to hear that Didier Drogba or Dean Karnazes had been there!)

As we went Krishnapur attempted to explain the concept of the various depictions of the gods Vishnu, Shiva and Kali; essentially the basic tenets of what is the 'Hindu' faith. To me though, as an untrained and uneducated westerner when it comes to Hinduism, when we got to the third representations it all became rather complicated and I struggled to follow what it all meant.

Walking down to the river I could see smoke trails drifting up to sky and the smells of incense. All along the banks were ghat's leading down to several platforms sat perched above the holy Bagmati river (disgusting and fetid – apparently it joins the Ganges further down). Pyres were stacked and bodies literally burnt wrapped in white shrouds. I watched as the families prepared the deceased, removing the clothes and washing them, it did not seem a particularly emotional experience as one would imagine and the way the body was handled was not as delicate as I would have thought. Once ready, an official from Pashupatinath in the role of 'Priest' appeared, I watched a few and it looked to be mostly teenage boys, probably holy men in training, who would circle the pyres and add bricks of something that appeared to be like firelighters. The families of the deceased had mostly shaved their heads, Krishnapur explained how the caste of the family dictated which platform you were cremated on be it the smallest at one end or the largest at the other. The caste system has been officially abolished in Nepal, supposedly. At one end of the river there was a group in military dress with seating nearby and a standing guard of armed soldiers and a band, a smattering of people around various mounds of smaller size had less fanfare. Krishnapur pointed further along the river, past the military funeral where there was an empty relatively clean space with little to no residue from cremation, this he said was for royalty only. The difference to Christianity in the approach to death was stark, here there were no tears and apparently little negative emotion. Even the approach to sex and intimacy was completely at odds with my Christian upbringing, it was these guys who invented the Karma Sutra, believing it important not to hide the body, but rather to explore it and all the sensations it can evoke and embrace it openly.

Sitting watching the bodies burn to ashes I was glad that in the west we don't take death so easily, in some ways I think to have such an outpouring of emotion is a good thing and says a lot about the void a loved one departing leaves behind. I wasn't so impressed with the way they just brushed the ashes into the 'Holy' river once the ceremony was over, it was just disgusting. Burial all the way for me.

Dotted about the whole are there were lots of Sadhus, holy men who were touting for pictures for a fee. Krishnapur explained these were the Hollywood element and that they have bad karma – he did not believe they would or could achieve Nirvana. He pointed out a window in a building across the river where a real sadhu sat perched looking down on the goings on below, he was an old disheveled semi-naked man. It was clear the difference between him and the more multicoloured and garish sadhus. The multi-colored ones were like the street performers you get in town centres back home.

We walked along the river to some caves set a little further up the river away from the funerary pyres, Krishnapur pointed out that there were many sadhus and gurus living within them from across the world, some were even from the UK and Austria, as well as a number of Buddhists. Clearly this was a holy place.

Pashupatinath had not been too high on my to do list, but had proved to be a thought provoking, interesting and spiritual experience, much enriched by my guide, Krishnapur. Although I was very disappointed at the end of my time with him when I gave him payment and he suggested it wasn't enough, destroying what I thought had been a good rapport. It was much more than the official guides cost.

As I left, I was sad to go, places that have a profound effect can be few and far between, I had genuinely been enraptured by the experience of Pashupatinath and had left looking to learn more about Hinduism.

Walking with Krishnapur had been such an interesting conversation, as well as discussing the temples and history of Pashupatinath, as so often happens we ended up talking about some of the issues facing his country. He told me that the period since the immediate aftermath of the earthquake had shown the failings of Nepal's system and infrastructure. He had been angered and frustrated that the well publicised aid money and resources were not being given back to communities or being invested in rebuilding. Since 2015, billions had been donated from across the globe, but this was hardly in evidence. He believed competing political views was the main issue, Maoists and city capitalists couldn't agree on anything leading to a stalemate. He made an ominous statement, that he believed if they couldn't sort their differences and focus on what was best for the people as opposed to their ideologies another earthquake would hit, that of the people. In Nepal, I could see nothing but entropy, time and nature slowly taking over, the state battered, used and worn. Take Pashupatinath for example, one of the worlds holiest Hindu shrines and Nepal's most important, it is quite literally crumbling to the ground, much like Durbar square, certain buildings have had to have been cordoned off with no visible signs of protection and being littered with debris, covered in filth and rubbish. Granted, it is a working temple, so much like a house that's lived in these temples are used, and one must remember that, but surely they could even use some of the ticket money to employ cleaners or 'tidiers', surely the people who see this river and this place as holy would want this? To protect it. To preserve it. To conserve it. Is it a lack of ambition or smarts? Are we in the West so different in our approach to living, life and the environment? Nepal really needs a kick up the bum, and being frank, help must start in the home.

Day 19 – Kathmandu

16/3/2016

I woke before 7:00am after a very deep and what felt like a very long sleep before heading out at 9:00am. Today I was going to Boudhanath Boudha stupa in the East of Kathmandu about 2.5km beyond Pashupatinath. Whereas the day before was a day for Hinduism, today was a day for Buddhism and Tibetan Buddhism at that.

In Thamel, I stopped for breakfast in the courtyard of a fairly decent hotel who served the popular Illy coffee. Perfect. It was not that early, so I was surprised to see so few people milling about, that was until I sat down and saw the infestation of flies. Now I am not really bothered by this kind of thing but quite a few of the other patrons seemed to be as they left their tables to head inside. I couldn't believe that for a country that has more than its fair share of flies due to their approach to waste management and hygiene, they don't seem to know how to deal with them. One waiter came along with a disgusting, fetid cloth to wipe down the table. Come on Einstein, the flies love the germs! How about some incense or even better a fly zapper – you know the one that goes 'bzzzzt'. A serious lack of common sense, or was it a lack of care? Or was it my western sensitivities to a handful of flies that the locals just don't get bothered by?

After breakfast I made my way to the stupa following the same route from the day before, to a point. After reviewing the map, I decided to take a little detour, but I don't think I gauged it quite right as a journey that should have been about an hour was pushing closer to two.

Wandering the countryside was lovely getting away from the worst of the traffic, I was lost in thought enjoying the scenery and apart from the odd car or truck, the relative peace and quiet. Then, all of a sudden, I was walking through what appeared to be a large, modern (in relative terms) housing development of three and four storey buildings painted all sorts of colours from greens, yellows, oranges and reds to pinks and blues. They were all extremely pretty and very much new, so much so that the roads and paths were still just dust tracks. Maybe this was an example of investment from the government? Maybe this was what they were going to provide for the displaced masses, new earthquake proof settlements? This was entirely at odds with what I had read about the area around the stupa of Boudha that was supposedly an area abundant with Tibetan exiles and refugees, monasteries with monks from across the world and the usual downtrodden that tend to congregate around the good and the generous.

I was sure I had gone wrong as I continued walking amongst the new, unoccupied neighborhood and asked the few people that I saw milling about where to go, it was lucky I did, as apparently I was a 10-15 minutes' walk too far south, this wasn't actually where I wanted to be. Clearly not, as there were no refugees nor exiles, only the scent of new development and comparative wealth.

After various wanderings in a northerly direction with the help of a lovely Tibetan lady who pulled me along confidently dropping me off at a local health clinic. I am not sure if she thought I needed help or I was going to help, in any case we smiled and said farewell as I followed her back out to the road wondering where the hell I was. Fortunately, a westerner in monks garbs came in my direction. She seemed deep in thought and we almost bumped into each other as I tried to get her attention. She too was absolutely lovely and took me with her along the road a couple hundred yards or so to the stupa area.

The monk had left me at the back end of Boudhanath but seeing as I knew I hadn't paid my entrance fee, which I knew was greatly needed I immediately headed round to the front and paid my 250R. Every little helps, even if deep down I knew not all the monies would end up where it should.

I walked back to rear of temple area where there was meant to be a peaceful garden and pool for contemplation, it turned out to be little more than a building site; I couldn't tell if it was due to earthquake damage or just a redevelopment program, I assumed it was due to the former. There was a depiction of Vishnu with his naga serpents at the centre of the pool, I could imagine the serpents being some sort of fountain and when completed it will be extremely impressive. I continued on the path working my way round to the front of the world heritage site stupa and was disappointed to see that it too, much like the pool, was little more than a building site, the spire had been removed for repairs and although the dome itself was undamaged the walls surrounding it which housed various smaller shrines were all in different stages of disrepair. I was sad, for the people, for the site and for myself. This was one of the things on the 'must see' list for Kathmandu, yet as it was, it was in barely working order and gave little hint as to the beauty and import this religious site once held. I went into the stupa and took what pictures I could but felt little of the overwhelming awe and sense of spirituality I had felt at some of the other sites on my trip.

I sat on a bench and watched the locals go clockwise around the stupa spinning their prayer wheels as they went and prostrating themselves. Mainly it was very old people, very few under 40s. The immediate area around the stupa had shops and restaurants with foods from all over the world and souvenirs for tourists. Apart from those circumnavigating the stupa there were few others praying, wrong time of day no doubt, apparently 4:00am and 3:00pm are peak times. For the first time in Nepal I had the feeling that this place was genuinely trying to capitalise on tourism, they seemed to have harnessed the wests fascination with Buddhism, packaged it in 'Om' trinkets and the like and were selling them to the masses.

Leaving my bench, I stepped into one of the many working monasteries in a building block surrounding the stupa, this had a great view and itself had marvelously painted murals and gilded ornaments. On the roof, for a few rupees you could light your own yak butter candle. Looking out over the Boudhanath area I was so disappointed. Whether it was due to the scaffolds, netting and building work or the unashamed tourism, I felt a lack of emotion or connection with the place, completely at the opposite end of the scale to what I had encountered in Durbar Square or Pashupatinath. A part of me felt that in this place, unlike the Hollywood sadhus at Pashupatinath, the effects of tourism had possibly unbalanced the local equilibrium tipping too far towards making money as opposed to enriching the soul.

I hasten to add, my view of proceedings was probably affected by the fact that I was sat there in the middle of the day and to get a full appreciation I should have joined at a prayer time. It did however seem that as it was, religion was closed for business and sellers and raconteurs had stepped in to fill the void.

Suddenly as I walked, I could feel a throbbing in my feet, they were bloody sore. The blisters on my toes were seething and I now didn't fancy walking back much, if indeed I would have been able to, so I grabbed a taxi, a Suzuki Maruti.

Someone deserves a big raise – all the taxis (and in fact pretty much 80% of all the cars) are Suzuki's. I wondered what lucky person negotiated this deal. Is the Maruti some mega efficient car? Cheap? (no doubt) or particularly suited to the undulating terrain and horrendous roads? Suzuki have either dumped stock surplus, or someone has taken a monumental backhander and kept Suzuki in the car business. The Maruti is definitely nothing special, a small compact car – utter shite in other words and if I could describe a suitable vehicle for these roads, the Maruti would be the most unsuitable car on all counts. However, my driver seemed more than happy, and his driving was phenomenal, maneuvering within millimeters between cars and people, even at slower speeds it was still terrifying with so many things to be aware of. At one point we came frighteningly close to a cow, and my driver quickly spun the wheel swerving out of the way. You have to love the Hindus, coming from a country like mine whose diet is largely beef to one where the cow is sacred always makes me smile – even the accidental death of such an animal could – in extreme circumstances lead to prison time of up to 15 years. The cows, as in this moment took on the role of Biblical Moses parting the automotive red sea (Stand next to a cow, it's the safest place to be!)

Moving past the cow my driver slammed his foot to the floor accelerating as he weaved between vendors, there really didn't seem to be any actual road rules. I sat in the front both impressed and petrified. As we pulled to a stop, I could feel the pulsating of my heart in my chest, no mistake, it had been exhilarating. Paying my money, I said as much to the driver who smiled and nodded enthusiastically. He had worn his belt the whole journey but told me on getting in I wouldn't need mine...

My day walking to Boudhanath had been largely a pleasant one, and indeed a surprising one, I had followed a lovely black relatively new asphalt paved road to get there, much like any back home, so the Nepalese do make roads. Which begs the question, why are there so few? Why isn't there a Ministry for infrastructure? Of course, I know there is one (Ministry of Physical Infrastructure and Transport, founded in 2000) but why are paved roads so uncommon, let alone flattened or prepared dirt tracks. Its not as if trucks and cars are uncommon. It seems that Thamel, Kathmandu and even Nepal are lacking a good, coherent and more importantly effective town planning department catering for roads, pavements or sidewalks. Sure it's a monster of a job for a country like Nepal, and after the earthquake they clearly have bigger fish to fry, but then again, of all times surely now, as they rebuild, is the time to look at planning, and forward planning at that for the future benefit of the nation. They could start in the suburbs like around Boudhanath and go from there because Thamel being so old and densely populated and developed would not provide the best canvas to begin with. Maybe that is what the new development I saw was the start of?

Day 20 - Kathmandu

17/3/2016

I had just been to the Palace Museum, the Narayanhiti Palace Museum to be more precise, and my immediate reaction was just 'wow'. Nothing like I had expected. The tour was little more than an hour, but it was memorable.

Designed by Californian architect Benjamin Polk in 1963 and completed in 1969, the Palace was a perfect recreation of that era, it was like traveling back in time. The interior reminded me of my Nan's old house and could be described as a bit chintzy. Inside and outside, a layer of dust coated everything, the sideboards, china, picture frames et al. It was as if the attempt to maintain it had gone too far so that now no one could go anywhere near anything and the city's smog was slowly starting to cover it all.

One would think a Palace should scream opulence, wealth and glamour, but this one fascinatingly was telling a tale of entropy and decay. The locals were fascinated and wandered excitedly, as no doubt a national of a country getting access to the hidden mysteries of the monarchy that had ruled their nation would. As a Brit, who also has grown up in a monarchy and enjoys a good palace I couldn't help but feel a little sad, this palace, in my opinion should be the literal jewel in the crown of the nation but was not much more than a fading, dilapidating tourist site. Disappointingly bags and cameras were not allowed.

In one room there were the gifts from other heads of state that had visited the Nepalese royals. I couldn't help but wonder if these were the actual gifts, replicas or if they had been planted to give an impression of importance and popularity. More than one statuette or painting had a name plate referencing a particular shop, studio or website...based in Thamel. I hoped it was simply that they had reproduced the replicas.

Most of the photos throughout were faded with age and the bookshelves held volumes from a different era including country guides, Agatha Christie novels and pulp fiction from the 50s and 60s. In the King's drawing room, there were souvenir plates; one that seemed to take centre stage had been a gift from Singapore bearing the image of the famous Merlion. To me, all these 'gifts', rather than suggesting importance and class, appeared a bit tacky.

As I walked around, I had to stop myself and consider whether it was me, being a snob. In the UK and Ireland, we have these old and grand palaces and castles that are protected and venerated and treated with utmost care and affection. We have trusts to protect them and encourage tourism that continues to fund the increasing costs of restoration and maintenance. However here, in Nepal's most important royal palace, bang in the heart of the capital, the place has been left to decay. I just couldn't understand the approach, or lack of. Even if the Royal family was overthrown in a revolution wouldn't they want to protect and maintain even for posterity? Let alone as a cash cow for tourism to boost the city coffers?

The brickwork of the main buildings had weeds peeping out and grasses were growing out of the guttering and roof slats. The 'gardens' were also in an unkempt fashion, clearly not having seen a gardener for some time. This was in stark contrast to the magnificent Garden of Dreams not 2 minutes' walk away. I pondered how the people could let this treasure begin to fall to ruin, especially as they see its value for tourism. Maybe it is because the revolution was so recent, the people might not have come to terms with the demise of Royal family and the events of the past twenty years, and until they do maybe they are unsure whether it is acceptable to be nostalgic. It may be that they rather than look at it fondly, it is more of a sideshow than a tourist site proper, to see where the gory events occurred on that fateful day on June 1st 2001, where a member of the royal family went on a killing spree murdering several. There are signs highlighting the bullet holes and where certain people were found, dead.

Overall, I was left feeling a bit sad, the palace should have been be the pinnacle and symbolic representation of a nation's wealth. The King had clearly maintained a wide variety of diplomatic relations (the Queen, Presidents of the USA, Ceausescu...) though the palace had little overt signs of a lavish lifestyle – or one that you would think befitted a head of state. Considering this, it may be due to a Buddhist/Hindu education which promotes spirituality above material possession, so in itself is not necessarily symbolic.

In the Kings lounge there was a TV and video recorder that apparently was a 'Sharp Dolby Surround' and on the walls were some very typical tourist prints of the English countryside, hardly portraits or landscapes by a master. Again, I wondered if this was the genuine palace interior of if, as I was starting to believe (and had been told by several people), after the massacre and revolution it was gutted by the revolutionaries and what we were walking around now was someone's view of what the palace interior should look like, having not seen the original. I couldn't believe that the royal family had lived in these buildings as recently as 2001, it was just so out of date.

I hope Nepal will learn to protect its fascinating heritage for future generations as the nation has a wealth of history to be enjoyed and learnt from – if maintained. As it was, like Boudha the day before and even Pashupatinath, there are lots of people ready to pay an entrance fee but little signs of it going towards conservation. Though I hasten to add that foreign restoration teams with their own funding are attempting to save several key places of historic interest, which is a start.

This day was to be my last before heading to Bhutan for a few days. I felt like I was done with Kathmandu, so the timing was just right. I was heading to Bhutan hoping to see something different, after that I would have a final couple of days for gifts etc. back in the Nepalese capital, but Bhutan was my last real experience in the true sense.

Nepal is and had been a fascinating place, it has everything you could wish for but on scratching the surface one can see it is held in a kind of limbo, stagnant and not going anywhere fast. With the lack of infrastructure, load shedding, inconsistent opening hours and the strange (to me) issues of caste, religion and diverse and extreme political spectrum all coming off the back of a major natural disaster it was no surprise the country felt shocked to a standstill.

The country has a pulse but felt like it needed a jumpstart. My guide at Pashupatinath said there was another earthquake coming...of the people; maybe, in a non-violent way, that is what is needed as no one seemed happy with the current situation but equally they accepted it as a 'fait accompli'.

The future does suggest massive investment from India and China which would help, but they themselves have competing interests and are not exactly paragons of virtue, headlining positive and healthy development.

Amazing place Nepal, I would watch their future with interest.

Day 21 - Nepal-Bhutan

18/3/2016

I couldn't sleep I was so excited. I spent way too long at the airport, but I didn't mind the wait – I was going to Bhutan!

As I sat there I had a flash of inspiration sadly a moment too late, I should have bought a Lonely Planet or something in the city, as my knowledge of the land of the Thunder Dragon was pretty much non-existent apart from a few tidbits of trivia such as changing from an absolute to constitutional monarchy in 2008 and the fact any visitor had to pay $250 per day surcharge to be escorted from arrival to exit. In the airport bookshop there was a copy priced up at 5000R, a quick bit of mental arithmetic and I realized this was roughly 30GBP – uhm no thanks.

At 9:30am we were called for boarding. I made my way with 39 others to the 'Druk Air' aircraft, a Boeing 319. The plane was almost empty apart from the smattering of foreigners, each with a row to themselves. From the takeoff I felt the journey was going to be something special as the plane sharply spiralled upwards to get above the smog line and then immediately veered off to the right-hand side, I could see the Himalayan mountains as clear as day. Who needed Tara Air and their sightseeing flights? Everest was there too, clear and majestic towering over the rest of the range, including my time at Kala Pattar this was the best view I had had, I snapped away with my camera delightedly.

Before we knew it, we began our descent and I recalled what I had read about Bhutan's Paro airport being among the world's most dangerous (in fact, some had this at number one!) According to the reports the takeoff and landings were such tricky maneuvers only 8 pilots knew the routine or flew it regularly. We suddenly banked sharply to the left and then to the right, it felt like the pilots had cut engines with the plane dipping sharply descending between some very imposing and seemingly very close hillsides. It was an experience.

The airport at Paro was strange. Indeed, my whole opinion of Bhutan from landing was of something very different and very old fashioned mixed with the here and now. From traditionally dressed men and women in clothes of fabulous colours and designs, glued to their iPhones, to buildings that from the outside looked like they were hundreds of years old but had such amenities as air conditioning, security cameras and internally were no different to what one would find in the west. And the place was just so quiet.

I exited arrivals and my guide welcomed me with a 'Mr. James' placard. It always makes me chuckle when I travel in Asia, the back to front nature of how they use names and surnames means you are often 'Mr. Michael' or 'Mrs. Michelle.' My guide was ChengGe and he was 25, or at least that's how it sounded, subsequently learned that is was in fact Cee Tshewang.

Initially I wasn't sure about his English and was very careful to grade mine, but before long we chatted away about many things and we quickly established that we shared the fact that we were both Chelsea fans and he had a particular interest in both Religion and Politics – perfect!

First on the agenda was lunch, we stopped on a street with a number of 2 and 3 storey buildings. There was a large temple to one side and every building had the traditional Bhutanese designs/murals. Tshewang told me that this was in fact enshrined in law, they had to look as they did. The roofs were made of sheet metal and were mostly green rested on wooden beams that protruded from just beneath through the walls. The tips were painted with floral designs. The decorations on the buildings tended to have the four friends design, the four friends being the elephant, monkey, hare and bird, representing harmony and cooperation and standing for the Bhutanese values of respect and generosity: and flying phallus's – yes, the phallus! Apparently, this holds special meaning in Bhutan, a means to ward off evil spirits and bad people. For an outsider it is quite a thing to be surrounded by so many erect penises, with wings and flames, depicted in quite some detail, although as with anything very quickly one becomes quite desensitised to it as the millionth flying phallus jumps out at you.

The whole place was incredibly tidy too, and I mean really tidy. There was no rubbish or litter and lots of bins not overflowing. Everything had the feel of being cared for, from the grass, to the sidewalks and flora and fauna. It was not what I expected, thinking the place would be more like what I had experienced in Nepal and Thamel, however it was a like show home version, a town before it had been properly lived in. Like something from the Truman show, a designer town. It was amazing.

The bottom floors of the buildings were shops of all sorts with mostly lodges, hostels, hotels and houses above. The streets themselves were quiet too, with barely any cars on the road and very little ambient noise apart from those of nature and the running water of the Paro Chhu river which flowed through the heart of the town; it was crystal clear and drinkable. Standing still you could even hear the odd bee or wasp; it was a little unnerving. The juxtaposition with Nepal was profound - this was Bhutan.

The second-floor restaurant was clearly for tourists, as I ascended the stairs I could see (and hear) an American family in one corner. Tshewang and I sat and ate together, whereas our driver, Kezang sat separately which surprised me, this though was going to be the norm apart from when I explicitly asked for otherwise.

The meal was served on individual dishes much like in China, the rice was a sweet red one, a cabbage and soy dish and a chilli beef dish that was particularly tasty. Tshewang pointed out a local delicacy called 'ema datshi' that was just to my liking. Chillis were cut and sliced then slathered in cheese sauce, mouth numbingly spicy but absolutely delicious. For my first experience of Bhutanese cuisine it was perfect, and I was impressed.

No sooner had I finished my second black coffee to wash down all the flavours and spice we were off site seeing, this afternoon there would be the National Museum, Kyichu Lhakhang Temple and Drukgyel Dzong.

My chauffeur driven Hyundai 4x4 set off to the first stop, the national museum.

As I watched the world go by, I asked Tshewang about what he and Kezang were wearing as they both were wearing traditional garb. Men wear what is called a Gho, a long robe similar to that of the Tibetan chuba, and women the Kira, a floor length patterned dress. Tshewang told me this was the equivalent of wearing a suit on formal occasions, which made sense as they were working, then he went on to clarify that this was also a period of national celebration so everyone was wearing their best - it wasn't just for me he smiled.

As we pulled up to the museum for some reason, I noticed that every car there, of which there were about twenty or so, was Japanese. I asked Tshewang why and he laughed acknowledging the point but didn't have an answer.

The National Museum of Bhutan is located on an outcrop overlooking a valley just above the Drukyel Dzong. 'Dzong' is the word for fortress, which is where all the regions administrations sit, a legacy from feudal society where the seat of power was a local dignitary's fortress or castle.

The Museum building was actually the 'Ta' of the Dzong, the watchtower. Owing to the number of earthquakes that strike the Himalayas yearly it is not unusual to see cracks zigzagging the walls and so it seems the locals have to renovate and rebuild as often as we paint back home; currently the tower was closed for re-construction due to the seasonal damage forcing the exhibits to be moved to a temporary building across the way from the tower.

The buildings were originally constructed in 1656 so to have withstood these centuries and still be in use (albeit not at that moment) was remarkable. As I was to discover most of the buildings in Bhutan were old, by that I mean 300-400 years on average and largely still being used, as if the whole country had frozen itself from modernity. This was one of the first obvious comparisons with Nepal who also, most notably recently, suffered at the hands of mother nature; but unlike their Himalayan neighbours however, appeared to have less regard for maintenance and preservation. Bhutan takes immense pride in its culture and fights to preserve it, shown in their approaches to tourism, education and the like.

It is so interesting that these two nations, both touching each other in the high Himalaya's, both relatively small, and both Buddhist and Hindu (each one or the other more so) have such different approaches to life and how they see their role in the world. They even share the same external forces of India and China.

My experience in Nepal had been one of utter frustration with the powers that be, especially since the earthquake and the lack of spending as the aid money continued to flood in. Bhutan however has nothing but absolute love and devotion for their monarchy and government. Allowing for the fact that I was being 'shepherded' around the land of the thunder dragon to see the absolute highlights and have a positive impression, the place seemed to evoke a feeling of contentment, satisfaction and happiness. The land that seems to measure success through the statistic of 'Gross National Happiness' seemed to be managing its modernisation gently, meshing the traditional and contemporary with comfort and ease. A lesson for many no doubt.

We had to wait outside the museum for a moment as I was informed that there were government visitors inside, probably checking on arrangements for the annual Paro 'Tsechu' that was to begin the next day for 5 days. It was a festival of dance mostly in celebration of the Bhutanese holy man, Guru Rinpoche, also known as the second Buddha.

As a steady stream of officials exited, I noted that they all wore scarf like things off their left shoulders, most wore white like Tshewang, but others wore all colours of the rainbow. Tshewang told me it was like a westerner wearing a tie, especially the white ones, though the more multicoloured ones tend to denote their status or position such as blue being worn by members of parliament, green for those in the legal profession and red and white by local politicians. I also noted some of the men had particularly decorative knee-high boots. These were considered the 'fancy' shoes for formal occasions. What I quite liked was that across this kaleidoscope of colour, it seemed that no colour nor pattern seemed off limits. No colour appeared to be particularly masculine or feminine with men wearing pinks. What surprised the most was when Tshewang told me that people loved wearing these clothes, even children. The gho and kira are considered peoples 'Sunday' best clothing but unlike back home where people feel that formal wear can be a bit stuffy the Bhutanese embrace every opportunity and enjoy wearing them. Each picture I saw of the beloved Royal Family showed they lived in these outfits, setting a good example. I had assumed, wrongly that people had to wear it almost begrudgingly and that they were not able to wear modern clothing, utterly incorrect. Bhutanese people savour their culture and take every chance to show the complexities, nuances and stark differences to the rest of the world with pride. From a young age they are educated (not indoctrinated) to embrace their unique culture and indeed seek to promote the values they hold in highest regard – a truly unique place in the world we live in today.

There is however, a blot in the history of this country of gross national happiness, something that is not openly discussed, and when it is, it is not seen particularly negatively by the locals; I found it hard to bring up with my very kind guide and driver. In 1988 a nationwide census was carried out, the purpose of which being to prove residence or claim to residence before 1958 i.e. citizenship. If not, as was the case for 80,000 Nepali settlers they were literally evicted from the nation based on fear of dilution of the Bhutanese culture. Those that could not prove Bhutanese heritage were held in refugee camps and continue to be 'settled' today in areas in northern Nepal, not officially recognized by either nation and for all intents and purposes, are stateless. A taint on this wonderful country and a nod to the negative effect absolute faith in nationalism can generate. The justification of this fear of dilution is so sad, it was the same justification the Germans used in the 1930s and the Chinese do today in the western provinces of China (Xinjiang, Tibet) that has caused such outrage across the world. To me, there can never be a justification for this kind of displacement.

Eventually we entered the museum but sadly no cameras were allowed. The museum was surprisingly detailed and interesting, much more so than I would have thought from the exterior. It gave an excellent overview of the country from the Thangkas (painted religious scrolls) dating back hundreds of years and the flora and fauna of the country (the national flower is a blue poppy, national animal a takin which is a type of goat/antelope that feeds on bamboo and lives at altitudes above 4000 metres). There were handmade sculptures of the Buddha and Guru Rinpoche as well as many painted ceremonial masks that were to be used in the national tsechu festivals, in fact these particular masks would be used in the tsechu I would see in the coming days.

The museum was excellent but did miss a couple of bits that I was hoping for. A bit about the history of faith of the nation, such as the influence of Guru Rinpoche and how this came about. The Bhutanese themselves take talking about their faith for granted like it is the most normal thing in the world, yet for a westerner couched in Christian faiths, Buddhism, although sharing much in common is a mystery. I made a mental note to speak to Tshewang and ask him as many questions as I could.

On the way to Drukgyel Dzong we passed through the valley and I had my first view of the Tigers Nest in the distance, the Tigers Nest being a Buddhist monastery clinging to the cliffside of the upper Paro valley. Words cannot describe the view or do it justice. This was on the list for the next day.

The road we followed wound through the valley into the hills, the beauty of the Bhutanese countryside and the neatly prepared agricultural land was breathtaking and like something out of a picture book. Despite the country being sat in the steep Himalayan range dense with hills and mountains, the people of Bhutan seem to be master cultivators, utilising all the available space making the most of the fertile basin forming a patchwork of greens and browns, the main crops being maize, rice and wheat. Here and there buffalo were walking and working, ploughing fields. Most animals, especially of the bovine variety, although not considered as sacred as back in Nepal, are kept for their ability to till the land and therefore are invaluable to the local populace and so treated with the utmost the respect, as are most animals in Bhutan.

However, dogs are another case entirely. As in Nepal there were stray dogs everywhere, reverting to their wolf-like instincts pottering about in packs whilst keeping an eye out for their next meal. These animals were ignored by the people, rather than being teased and treated with disdain. In

Bhutan they are rarely acknowledged, like butterflies, birds and insects, they are just there. According to Tshewang the reason there are so many is that animals are not spayed in Bhutan, so when they have big litters the people just don't keep them, and so they are set free.

Buildings dotted the landscape in a very haphazard manner without any apparent rhyme or reason. The houses were family homes and were generally larger than a typical western house. I asked if generations lived together which would explain the multiple storeys as well as the apparent size of the dwellings, Tshewang said not, they just have big houses, lots of space, I guess.

Driving through the valley I was struck by the feeling that although there were man-made dwellings and indeed man had cultivated the land, sculpting it for their needs, there was a sense of harmony and balance, complimenting each other. We in the west have started to see nature in this way, but we acknowledge more could be done to pay attention to this balance. According to Tshewang this balance contributes quite heavily to the 'gross national happiness' and thence productivity and therefore self-fulfillment.

The Dzong, or fortress we headed to was also sat on a hill overlooking the valley on the main road to Tibet. It had been built in 1649 to commemorate a victory over their neighbours to the north and as a fortress to defend against further incursions. The design had a clever second entrance that was seen as the main by way by outsiders, it lured them into a central courtyard that effectively penned them in ripe for picking off. Tibet and Bhutan have had a history of strife due to the religious differences between the Gelugpa (Tibetan) and Nyingma (Bhutanese) sects of Buddhism. Buddhist war? Even a way of life that professes peace is not immune from man's inhumanity to man.

Since the 17th century the Dzong had become less of a fortress and more of a trading post and administration centre for the area until 1951 when a butter lamp caught fire and all but destroyed it leaving it in the condition that I found it. Tshewang said there were talks of renovation but as it was almost a complete ruin it was more of a rebuild than a renovation. The char marks were still clear on the internal walls where the fired had raged over sixty years ago.

Unfortunately, as we approached, we could see that the doors were locked so I couldn't go into the main courtyard and managed only to peer through cracks in the outer masonry. It was an interesting building, much like a castle although it didn't appear as robust in the sense of the materials used for construction, the stones were of all shapes and sizes and mixed into a packed earth. After a few photo moments involving the valley, a snow-capped mountain and the remains of Drukgyel Dzong, we made our way to the next stop on the itinerary, Kyichu Lhakhang, an extremely old working temple.

The drive was pleasant along a paved and new single-track road, speeds and progress were slow. The sides of the roads displayed some amazing signs, not your atypical road signs but fantastic slogans like 'if you are married, divorce speed' – love it.

We passed a number of men practicing archery dressed in their gho's, it was a stark juxtaposition to see them with light ultra-modern bows made from carbon fibre. Archery is the national sport of Bhutan and it seemed this group had set up an impromptu competition by the side of the road. The target was a standard size maybe 150 feet away. They attached coloured fabric to their arrows and would take it in turns to fire at the quite small, and quite distant target. The skill was frightening, especially as people at the target end stood literally next to it unafraid of a stray arrow – I wonder how many accidents occur?

Whoosh – the arrows flew with incredible speed, so much so I couldn't follow with my eye but could tell by reactions at the target end when people would remove the shaft leaving the coloured ribbon where it fell to show where it had landed, most were hitting the target. Tshewang told me that the best archers were both rich and famous.

There was another group huddled and crouched playing dice for money, uninterested in the show of skill on the other side of the road, they were gambling on luck. Laughing and joking they asked if I wanted to join, I politely declined, I have never been great at gambling. All the men had red stained teeth and lips, this was because of 'doma', a combination of a crushed areca nut and lime powder wrapped in a leaf, it has narcotic properties; I had seen it before in other east Asian countries. The taste is meant to be bitter and not only makes the mouth red but the spit too, much like blood, not very attractive. A smiling gentleman offered me some, again I declined. We hopped back in the car and resumed our journey.

Kyichu Lhakhang temple is said to have been built in the year 659AD by Songtsen Gampo, the then king of the Tibetan Empire which encompassed the area of Bhutan as well as Nepal and large swathes of China. Many outer buildings had been added on to the original as well as new artistic adornments such as gilding and murals as recently as 1968, it is a living, working centre still. The original temple is held to be one of 108 built across the Tibetan Empire by the king as part of an attempt to subdue an ogress who was stopping Buddhism take hold as she was laying over the top of Lhasa, the capital. I do love these views of history that mix myth, legend and truth much like Geoffrey of Monmouth's account of Britain and King Arthur, myth and fact weaved with artistic flair. A fair few Bhutanese believe the stories and history to be true, one person at Kyichu Lhakhang told me that the temples role specifically was to help pin the left leg of the ogress.

Inside the main temple was a statue dedicated to the revered second Buddha, Guru Rinpoche of Bhutan. Tshewang prostrated himself three time touching his head, mouth and heart and made a small donation. He encouraged me to make a wish, not for myself but for mankind as per a Bodhisattva (a hero of enlightenment) seeking compassion for mankind. This I did as well as make a small donation, but didn't feel right prostrating myself, I didn't want to be a fraud.

Temples in Bhutan were each very similar in overall design with fabulously colourful murals at the entrances of the gods of the north, south, east and west. There were a thousand gold buddha statuettes lining the walls with various tables and altars holding offerings and flowers; and of course, in the centre of each temple would be a massive gold representation of Guru Rinpoche. It is important to note, Buddhas are not gods themselves, they are simply enlightened beings sharing their teachings on how best to live or be, much like a priest or a monk, not a god. A common misconception.

There is, therefore, compatibility between Buddhism and other faiths, be it Hinduism as in Nepal, or even Christianity in the West, the foundation tenets of peace, love and charity are universal. Tshewang advised I check out a book called 'What makes me not a Buddhist' – which although a statement is a rhetorical one that could be ended with a question mark. The gist being that it says everyone has the potential for Buddhahood, or to be enlightened. It is just about living and being good and trying to be the best we can be. Sounds quite familiar to sainthood.

Walking outside there were 3 huge prayer wheels which as with all, had to be walked around in a clockwise fashion. An old man (seriously old!) was shuffling holding some prayer beads, much like a rosary, chanting the mantra 'om mani padme hum' spinning the wheels inscribed with the same mantra. I asked Tshewang how often he would come and do this and even how many times he might have done it, he responded uncountable times. For some people this was all they did. To see such genuine devotion was humbling.

It was now early evening, so we left for the hotel, a so called 3-star establishment but in reality, far better, Mandala hotel overlooking the stunning views of the Paro valley. In Bhutan, when like me you are on a fixed tour, foreigners tend to stay in the same places, in fact they must. For me this was okay especially as the standards were so high. After Nepal, to have electricity, a bath, satellite television with BBC World News and a clean comfortable bed with such amazing views of the Dzong was a treat. The buffet food was pretty good too. Considering I had only been in Bhutan half a day, the day rate of $250 I considered well spent. The next day was the actual reason I had come to Bhutan, to see one of the 'new' wonders of the world, the Tigers Nest temple. I genuinely couldn't wait.

Day 22 - Paro – Bhutan

19/3/2016

We drove about twenty minutes to Taktsang Goemba – the Tigers Nest.

Paro and its valley really are incredibly beautiful, farmland and forest without the noise of life and industry. Even the woods themselves appear quite mystical with varieties of trees very different to those we have in Britain, engulfed in a light mist in the cool morning.

We parked up at what I imagine was the car park, although at this stage there were no others we could see. I leapt out of the car and we started up the trail. Within a few moments we peaked a small crest and I spotted a row of souvenir sellers at what might have been the entrance to the trail proper, even in this haven of Bhutan they know the value of tourism.

Tshewang said the hike would take between 1.5 to 2 hours, depending on me and how leisurely or strenuously we were going to take it. For me, I was feeling the elevation already, Paro was 2200m above sea level, and in spite of my Everest adventure I still found it quite hard going, and moreover I could hear Tshewang struggling to keep up with my early pace. Maybe walking alone in the Himalayas had encouraged me to plough on, but in this serene environment I just wanted to savour it and so took my foot off the gas. My natural instinct is to always go 100mph, to get where I am going and then relax, though if Sagarmartha taught me anything it is the value of pacing.

The trail wound steadily up the hillside, though the footing was not always easy with surface dusting, tree roots and stones dotted about. I imagined the rain season and the monsoons they brought thinking they would make the trail nigh on impossible to climb.

In the distance I spied someone coming down the trail, it was an older British gentleman looking very pale. It seems we weren't the first on the trail that morning, which surprised me as we had walked for a good twenty or so minutes without seeing anyone. The man had collapsed further up and had decided to head back to a lower elevation leaving his party to push on. By the top we would be at near 3000m and for those unacclimated this can prove physically challenging, as in the case of this gentleman. He stopped to rest, so we pushed on after confirming he was okay.

We passed more tourists as we carried on, although I had cut my pace, we were still going at a good clip winding through the prayer flag filled forest. I noted that all we passed were a lot older than myself (probably why we were passing them all!) and indeed throughout my time in Bhutan that was the general way of it. There were of course lots of tourists but only a handful around 30. It seems the cost of visiting does restrict the casual backpacker in favour of the high value tourists – a genuine intention of the Bhutanese government and tourist bureau.

An hour or more passed and we continued ever up chatting away. We stopped at a bench that had been placed offering stunning views of the nest between a cleft in the mountains, that is, if it weren't for the morning mist. A couple of other people were there contemplating turning back due to the altitude and the effect it was having on them, disappointed by their 'lack' of view at the bench as they were hoping that had they seen the nest, they could have turned back happily.

Positively, I urged them on telling them that the view would only get better the further they went and that as the morning warmed the mist would dissipate. I don't think they appreciated a young upstart driving them higher up into the mists, although fortunately, I wasn't wrong to suggest a little further would be better views, as within minutes there was another small plateau with prayer wheels and a café, itself offering stunning views especially as the mists drifted apart on occasion to the audible 'oohs' and 'aahs' of the tourists. I needed the bathroom, so a pit stop presented an opportunity for a coffee and biscuits.

Finishing my coffee I was eager to carry on, speaking to a Hungarian tourist (who I would meet later on in Bhutan, most tourists have the same or similar schedules) he told me a story of a Thai lady who had died falling off the paths up to the monastery. This was a bit out of the blue as we had just met and this was his opening gambit, after the typical where are you from question. It was a bit morbid and a bit of a downer considering I was so excited to be where I was. It did however awaken my senses to the dangers of hiking in the mountains and that no matter how seemingly safe you are you must always keep your wits about you. Note to self, always look where you are going.

Onwards we went until the path finally began to level out and a large flagpole poked its head up on the horizon with billowing prayer flags hanging off it. Approaching I was blown away, my first clear view of the monastery was incredible. Being built into the face of the cliff its sheer presence seemed implausible, how had they done it? Especially considering it was done in the 17th century! The white and red building jutted out looking down over the Paro valley, clinging to the rock, nestled in the crags, nooks and crannies. It looked just amazing. Needless to say, this was THE picture moment.

It was here that Tshewang gave me a brief history of Taktshang Goemba. Built in 1692 it had survived a series of fires, one as recent as 1998 that had almost completely destroyed the main structure meaning it had to be largely reconstructed before reopening for use in 2005. The building as it was didn't look like it was from 2005, which was nice; clearly, they were trying to retain the traditional feel. The monastery was dedicated to Guru Rinpoche who reportedly flew to a cave on the mountain on the back of his consort, a tigress, initially to subdue a local demon and then to meditate for 3 years and 3 months. Looking at the caves on the face of the rock from where I stood, they even made the face of an angry faced Buddha adding weight to the story, or was this just a trick of the eye? Also, apparently in the cave of the main temple in the monastery you can see the outline on the rock of a meditating Guru Rinpoche. Whether you believe the myths surrounding the nest or not, the place was definitely a holy place for Buddhists. Even for non-Buddhists like myself, the Tigers Nest has an aura and presence, possibly due to the spectacular setting that engenders a notion of respect and spirituality. I couldn't help but wonder, how had they even transported materials back in 1692? The journey up from the valley was certainly not easy, and that was for a 33-year-old carrying a small backpack, for those that built it, it was an incredible feat of man.

From where we were, to get to the nest we had to descend the left-hand side of the cliff which then wrapped around and back up the other side. Here the danger of falling was ever present and made me think of the story of the Thai lady, it wouldn't have surprised me had she fallen somewhere near here.

As we walked all that could be heard was the rush of the wind blowing into the rocks and around the cliffs and the steady flow of running waterfalls out from the caves and gaps in the rocks.

In a cleft near the lowest point before heading back up to Taktshang Goemba there was a small temple dedicated to the 'tigress' consort Yeshe Tshogyel, known as 'Snow Lion Cave' (Singye Pelphu Lhakhang). Tshewang stopped for a moment before we carried on, I wasn't sure if he was praying, probably just paying his respects. We then headed up the pretty steep and slippery stairway to the nest proper.

I wasn't aware at the time, but entrance to the nest is only permitted if your guide has pre-arranged your visit. One can't just arrive and buy a ticket. Tshewang had already sorted ours but sadly no cameras were permitted inside, this seemed to be the norm in Bhutan, no doubt due to the fact that these were revered sites, much as we do in the west in some places. It is a shame though as it would be great to share with people these unknown and yet fabulous interiors with the amount of solid gold statues, gold leaf and stunning murals. They would put even the most opulent Cathedrals to shame.

We went through the various rooms and I just tried to take it all in, the amount of detail was overwhelming everywhere you looked. Tshewang prostrated himself in the main room in front of the statue of Guru Rinpoche and donated, I felt it right to give a donation and made a private wish that was allowed, so Tshewang said. Everywhere there were monks chanting unconcerned and oblivious to the tourists wandering about, of which there weren't too many to be honest. I asked question after question utterly fascinated by this Buddhism, different to my limited firsthand experience and perception, I was now seeing it all around me living and breathing. It was something I hadn't seen like this before, so raw and so real. I wanted to know more, about the history, the meaning, the philosophy. Tshewang gladly answered all my questions telling me the about demons covering the Himalayas and the flying Guru Rinpoche, at no point did he refer to the stories as myths but as a real history of Buddhism and the region.

I spoke to a British man at the main door on the way out who was a hiking tour leader. He had first been to Bhutan in 1995, very early in the countries process of opening up and he said that the Bhutan I was seeing was now unrecognisable from that which he had experienced all those years ago. That Bhutan had developed and industrialised far beyond what he had fallen in love with. From what I could see the country was still in the early stages of development in terms of infrastructure, he suggested that not all development is good and was regretful that they had even gone as far as they had. I didn't get time to probe him further as he had to leave. I was intrigued as my experience so far, although limited was of a country that was trying and succeeding in balancing modernisation and the associated benefits of electricity, running water, transport and infrastructure as well as maintaining their respect and appreciation for their culture and the environment. I had just arrived though, and he had had many years of experience, however I couldn't help thinking that he had such a romantic view of this 'Shangri-La' that he would prefer it to have stayed the way it had for his idyllic notions of a forgotten kingdom.

I collected my bag and camera and turned back one last time to gaze at one of the world's true wonders. Walking back the way we had come we passed a growing number of people coming the other way, looking at their puffed out faces and at those that had paused, usually bent over on the brink of turning around I would offer them encouragement telling them it was definitely worth it, to come to this place and not see the Tigers Nest would be criminal. We passed several people who had evidently decided that hiking was not for them and so were on horseback – not a bad idea.

Tshewang and Kezang (my driver) had decided to switch the schedule around, so we would instead head to the capital Thimphu today before returning to Paro the next day as the festival that was going to happen at the Dzong would be very interesting and they didn't want me to miss it, I am pretty sure they didn't want to either. So, after a delicious lunch, a cross between momo and Chinese dumplings, we headed to Thimphu.

The distance from Paro to Thimphu is not actually that far running at about 50km. However, the nature of the road (and mostly lack thereof) and the mountains mean this journey can take anywhere upwards of two hours. Beware anyone afraid of heights or who suffers mountain sickness as at times the tarmac of the road goes right to the edge and it feels like you are inches from oblivion.

Thimphu is a city of only about 100,000 people and unlike Paro which is spread throughout a fertile valley is rectangular and feels more 'designed' than organic. The palace and administrative buildings sit at one end with the long thin city running off it, very different to a typical radial layout.

The city has not always been the capital of Bhutan, it changed from Punakha during the reign of the 4th King in 1962. With the active opening of the country it was felt that Punakha, not too far from Thimphu as the crow flies, was too remote in terms of access. Sadly, I wasn't going to be able to visit that city on this trip.

The capital was similar in many respects to Paro, but nowhere near as aesthetically pleasing. Thimphu is a mix of modern and traditional with numerous nightclubs, restaurants and coffee shops along Norzin Lam, the High Street. Interestingly I didn't see any 'brand' shops, all were independent, though like Nepal I did see one or two signs for Illy coffee, their Asia sales team had really earned their pay and clocked up the airmiles.

Also, like Nepal, with India being the biggest trade partner it is not uncommon for many high-end items only to be available from shops via import from India such as iPhones and the like. I often wondered in both countries how long it would be before brands finally made there moves into these markets.

The first stop in Thimphu was Motithang Takin Preserve, or better known as, the zoo. Essentially it was a large pen with lots of takin and deer. It looked like they were in the middle of development so maybe one day they would expand into other Himalayan animals. For a country and region blessed with such a variety of flora and fauna native to such small areas it would be incredible for them to have a Himalayan specific zoo showcasing snow leopards, tigers, rhino or elephant. Then again, putting such magnificent beasts in pens is probably contradictory with the Bhutanese view of the world and environment.

The takin is quite an interesting animal, there is a humorous tale about how it was created by the Lama Drukpa Kunley, the so-called Divine Madman in the 15th century. Apparently, he ate a whole goat and a whole cow and merged the bones to form the takin. Bear in mind, this animal, at full height is absolutely massive.

After, we headed to a textile museum, this was the token 'factory' of any guided tour where they show you around all the handcrafts and ask you to buy something. It was closed. Changing our schedule meant that we had arrived too late, Tshewang was disappointed for me, I wasn't.

Instead we scooted off to Trashi Chhoe Dzong, the religious and administrative centre of the country housing the National Assembly, National Council, the residence of the Chief Abbot, the King's office and a surprisingly small Royal Palace. We were only allowed into the Dzong which itself was incredible, just the sheer scale of it and the deafening silence. Seeing as I am fascinated by politics not to be able to tour the parliament house was a disappointment, so I had to settle for photos of the outside.

Bhutan is an interesting case study in the modern world, of how to change, develop and grow peacefully and united in a cause. Having only transitioned from absolute monarchy to constitutional monarchy in the late 1990s in such a peaceful way, that the monarchy is still absolutely adored by the population in incredible and almost unbelievable – and yet it is genuine.

The political system in Bhutan is not too dissimilar to the UK with an upper and lower house in parliament, though the King still holds a lot of influence unlike the UK. I tried to gleam the differences from Tshewang between the different bases of political thought, but he just kept reiterating that one group just sits in opposition – opposition to what? From talking generally, I think that the majority of people are conservative in the traditional sense, not liking radical change, but very socially aware. It made me smile when Tshewang told me that during the transition of the monarchy in the 90s the people even sent a letter to the King asking him if they could refuse the proposed changes to a constitutional monarchy, they were trying to refuse franchisement! The King denied them, saying it was in their interest to move towards democracy – what a man.

Day 23 - Thimphu – Paro

20/3/2016

The hotel again was very nice, it had no bath which was a shame, for some reason I kind of expected one, but I did manage to watch Chelsea on Star TV (BT equivalent from India). This was a pleasant surprise and more than I would get where I was staying in Nepal. It's a shame that I would not have time to really appreciate these hotels as they were a very high standard and I only had a few days in the country.

First stop after breakfast was the Tibetan styled National Memorial Chorten built in memory of the 3rd King in 1974, a chorten being another name for stupa, the mound like/hemispherical structures that housed relics and used for meditation. The people adored the 3rd King too, he began the process of opening the country having seen the threat of an expansionist China that had invaded Tibet in the 1950s. He realized that by plugging into the global system they might be afforded an element of protection if only by being known on a world stage. He also knew that any opening up would also lead to change. He tried to ensure that any change was measured, managed and always with an eye on protecting the 'National Identity'.

We left the hotel quite early and already people were circumambulating with their prayer beads chanting mantras. They were mainly older people, retirees and the elderly. Apparently, these people would come daily when their children would drop them off before work and collect them after. Young people would pray less, mainly at home, but as they got older (or nearer death as Tshewang said) they generally feel the need to do it more. I think for my father and especially my grandmother's generation this was also true for Catholics, less so nowadays. The people would circle the chorten hundreds and maybe thousands of times per day just because they felt the need, just because it made them feel better providing some inner peace, how wonderfully devout.

Next was probably the most amazing thing in all of Thimphu.

Driving up into the hills overlooking the city not only were met with superb views but there was also the most incredible 50ft statue, the Buddha Dordenma. It was made of gold and Bronze plate and paid for by a Hong Kong based benefactor just for the benefit of mankind. It was just magnificent.

Beneath the statue there were going to be numerous chapels housing some 100,000 smaller statuettes, but as yet the site was still unfinished and under construction. In scale and scope, I can only compare it to Cristo Redentor on the Corcovado mountain in Rio de Janeiro. This statue, like Christ the Redeemer in Brazil, completely dominated the Thimphu skyline. It was a remarkable thing glinting in the sunlight and is an extraordinary place that is starting to gain a reputation as the 8th wonder of the modern world.

All too soon it was time to leave the capital and begin the bone jarring and stomach-churning journey back to Paro and the Tsechu Festival at the Paro Dzong.

As we drove into Paro, the place was unrecognizable from what we had left the day before, it was so busy with thousands of flags, multi-sized and multicoloured hanging on bamboo canes either sides of the roads and paths up to the courtyard/square where the dancing and festivities were to be held. There were cars 'everywhere', which surprised me from how few and quiet it had been the day before (still all Japanese) and all the locals were now wearing their traditional fineries, a true kaleidoscope of colours. It was now that I really noticed how many Indians and Nepali there were mixed in the population as they tended to wear their day to day clothes, like me, looking very shabby in my beard, boots and hiking clothes.

To get to the parade ground we had to cross the crystal-clear Paro Chhu river, Tshewang had mentioned it was drinkable and seeing it glint and twinkle in the daylight I believed him, it was free from pollution. The river was spanned just below the Dzong by an old styled bridge (Nyamai Zam). Tshewang told me it was hundreds of years old, which I readily accepted as it didn't look very new, though a little research later I discovered the original had been washed away in floods in 1969 and so was now a reconstruction, styled to look aged like the old one. It looked good though, and sufficiently distressed and rickety, reminiscent of something out of Harry Potter and Hogwarts.

We followed the path mingling with the locals and other tourists; the excitement was palpable. I had the feeling that this was a major event on the annual calendar, and I was getting sucked in eagerly anticipating what I was going to see having very little idea apart from a few photos and bits I had read. Tshewang informed me that this event was so big that in fact people from all over the country would be attending. It turned out that the next day even he King and his family would make an appearance. On my way to the airport we passed the cavalcade of Mercedes'.

After crossing the bridge, we first turned left to head into the Dzong for a quick look, it was far more beautiful than the one in Thimphu, the colourful flags for the festival no doubt added to the splendor. Here Tshewang attempted to teach me about the wheel of life and the six forms of existence, a main tenet of Buddhism. Again, a bit like at the Tigers Nest and the story of Guru Rinpoche he seemed to take the concept of rebirth and the modes of existence literally whereas I looked at it more allegorically. Having said that, I am sure any agnostics or atheists would think the same way about my faith as a Catholic. Still, I was absolutely fascinated and coming to like a lot of the ideas behind Buddhism without too many contradictions with my own faith, note to self – investigate further.

We left the Dzong and went up to the parade ground composed of a flat area off to the side of the main building. There were literally hundreds of people milling about, all dressed in fabulous colours. On two sides of the square was a two or three storeyed building that was the living quarters of the local monks, they were like ants poking their heads out of all the windows to get a good view of the events below. On another side a little back from the square was a covered stand, police were moving people so as to clear a view to the parade ground, as the stand was just off the floor and not sufficiently high to see over standing people. This area was reserved for dignitaries and Royalty.

I looked around and noted all the different scarves of office, the different types of footwear and jewellery, it really was a magnificent sight especially to see people from all parts of Bhutanese society sharing in the same festival, celebrating, laughing and playing. The spectacle made me think of medieval tourneys, sadly back home there are very few events of this kind, a modern equivalent would be summer festivals, although these seem to draw a particular type. It was clear for me to see that this kind of event could only be a positive thing to bring a community together.

I sat down with the other spectators, Tshewang and Kezang left me to it as they went to catch up with friends, as everyone near or far was present they were taking the opportunity. I didn't mind being left alone and in fact enjoyed just soaking up the atmosphere. In the few hours we were there I only managed to see one official dance; the rest were of 'clown' type characters entertaining the audience with silly walks and slap stick. There are eight official dances in honour of the eight manifestations of Padmasambhava, another name for Guru Rinpoche. I did see part of the Black Hat Dance, which is one of the eight dances, it is about removing obstacles for oneself in life; it ran on for some time, apparently in Tibet it can last for days.

The Tsechu (Dzongkha), or festival was going to run for 5 days in Paro, others are of varying length at different times across the country. The length meant they could spread out all the main performances and intersperse them with other entertainments be it for audience participation, education or sheet comedic value. These lulls in action allowed for the social aspect of the gatherings, as well as trade and business opportunities. As Bhutan is so spread out and villages so remote without roads and many cars, the Tsechus provide a good opportunity to take care of a multitude of bits and pieces.

Initially, I thought it was all just fabulous, especially the dance itself. The clowns, after a time were a little tiring, especially when there were not many clues as to what was going on. Everyone else seemed to get it though, it must have been my lack of Bhutanese, but every so often the crowd would break out into raucous laughter, clapping hands and slapping thighs enthusiastically. There was a man on a microphone somewhere at the back, I supposed acting as a kind of master of ceremonies, probably giving muffled commentary to keep everyone in the know. Throughout however I could see many drift off into conversation or tuck into huge homemade picnics groups of families had brought. Interestingly, around the square I couldn't see anyone selling local foods. It all gave me a true sense of what the Tsechu was about, the events in the square were a constant over the days of the festival, and it was not considered unacceptable to dip in and out, much like having a radio on in the background, of course the main 'Cham' or masked and costumed dances were always well attended .

Just as I was about to leave, I bumped into the Hungarian man I had spoken to on the hike up to the Tigers Nest. We chatted briefly; he said he had enjoyed the beauty of Bhutan but did not appreciate the fact that one had to be part of a guided tour, albeit a relatively small group (single person with guide and driver). He was a staunch independent traveler and begrudged the lack of freedoms to explore. His background was that he had left Hungary under communism and now split his time between Brazil, Thailand and the Philippines and told me openly he was a sex tourist – it didn't surprise me from his holiday destinations and although I didn't agree with his life choices I liked his candour. I asked him where next and he said Tibet. If he didn't like a tour led trip he was in for an interesting time, I wished him good luck, like Bhutan it is the only way into Tibet currently with a government issued travel permit via government affiliated travel groups.

Day 24 – Bhutan – Kathmandu, Nepal

21/3/2016 Paro

After a lovely breakfast it was time to say farewell to Bhutan. I bade Tshewang and Kezang a sad goodbye, they were both absolutely lovely and been worth every penny of the $250 daily fee. They kindly said I had been unlike any foreigner they had met and a very special human being, this choked me a bit and I was touched. We parted ways and I went to queue up at the airport.

I will stay in contact with Tshewang, rarely do you meet people you can tell are completely genuine and pure. He was just so kind. One day, if God wills it, I will return to see more of that fabulous country and hopefully share it with my family, it is a very special place I feel privileged to have experienced just a small part of.

Once back in Kathmandu I checked back into the guesthouse and had a quick nap before heading out for a coffee. I hadn't done any real writing whilst in Bhutan, the days were so full and I had felt exhausted in the evenings, so I decided I would spend my final couple of days in Nepal catching up and reflecting. The afternoon flew by and before long it was night, so I headed back to the guesthouse.

I was finally starting to feel unplugged from the system, as if the weeks I had been without phones or computers had really done me some good. I was starting to think about bigger picture items, life, choices and the experiences I had gone through, though most importantly – who did I want to be. Having been blown away in Bhutan by the simplicity of life it had raised some important questions and lessons about how to take back my life and move forward after a difficult period. All quite deep thoughts for a Wednesday afternoon.

Day 25 - Kathmandu Nepal

22/3/2016

Holi!

I had planned to head into the mountains to visit a couple of temples and shrines today but no sooner did I head outside than some children (and adults) were throwing coloured powders and water at me. A lady came up and put a tikka on my forehead and told me that there was to be a large party in Durbar Square later in the day. I would think about heading there after my hike, mentally though I was in a space where I wanted to be alone, and Holi is not one for isolation.

Holi is a Hindu festival to celebrate the oncoming cool monsoons and is absolutely crazy, there is no escape. The excitement on everyone's faces was brilliant. Children were off school and small shops were closed, it felt like everyone was outside going mental. The general traffic seemed to be a lot lighter too matching the fact that many people weren't working. Saying that though, there were still hordes of mopeds overladen with people (and goods) tooting and shouting. As I walked from the guesthouse gangs of people were singing and laughing with music blaring everywhere. It felt like Nepal had come alive today in a way I hadn't seen yet, it seemed that the festival was an opportunity to let their hair down and the atmosphere had changed from one of slight tension and frustration to being overwhelmingly positive.

I grabbed a taxi to take me to Kopan Monastery as it was a bit far for a walk, the driver asked if I didn't like crowds as he couldn't understand why I was heading out of town when I was in the heart of the festivities in Thamel. He said Holi was a time to be happy and with other people; as we drove to the hills I could see everyone seemed to agree with him as coloured powders filled the air with the incessant sound of horns and people singing 'happy happy Holi!' It was the same no matter how far from Thamel we were, just less foreigners.

As I sat back watching this all I couldn't help feeling outside it all, like a voyeur, it was fascinating yes, and in another time, in a different mindset I would have been all for it to, but to be truthful I really just wanted to visit the monastery and have some quiet time.

Kopan Monastery was my first stop, north in the hills of Kathmandu. The monastery followed the Gelugpa tradition, the dominant school of four schools of Tibetan Buddhism, the others being Nyingma, Kagyu and Sakya. The teachings are the same, differing only in emphasis such as Gelugpa focusing on study and discipline in life and action, whereas Kagyupa focuses on meditation for example. An interesting side note is that the Dalai Lama is always a Gelugpa.

At first it looked like the monastery was closed as I peered through the locked gates. Then all of a sudden, a small door opened in the large wrought iron and a security guard stepped out to welcome me in.

The buildings were decorated beautifully with painted murals containing quotes by eminent people such as the 14th Dalai Lama (Lhamo Thondup, the current Lama in exile in India). From the center of the compound you could see out over the city and it afforded probably the best and clearest view I had experienced in my time, from other locations there had always been a heat haze or some pollution but today, looking southwards, Kathmandu looked stunning with its multicolored and multi storeyed buildings. It was also very hot, and the sky was very blue.

Walking around there were so many bushes, flowers and trees, all at once looking both organically situated and yet perfectly maintained. It is no surprise to me that this is such a popular retreat destination, as I thought this whilst wandering through one of the gardens I spied a monk in robes having a sit down with a group of foreigners of all ages and apparently all nationalities. I eavesdropped for a moment; he was teaching meditation. Fascinated as I was, I considered it rude to gatecrash so carried on my private tour.

Next, I went towards the main temple building, I could hear the chanting of the monks and approaching I could see them sat cross legged in their rows in front of a large statue of Gautama Buddha. Again, they seemed of all ages but also focus, as some just looked around or sat staring in silence. I asked a monk in passing how often they would do this; he said all day 5 days a week. No wonder I thought that some were looking bored, and it was only Tuesday.

Leaving the monks to their study I felt at peace, this place felt a world away from the hustle and bustle of Kathmandu and listening to chanting can be extremely hypnotic. It was calming and therapeutic to just stand there.

I noticed a sign for a bookshop just over to one side of the courtyard, I couldn't leave without a look. I dug out the book that Tshewang had mentioned – 'What makes me not a Buddhist' and gladly handed over my £3.

Kopan was such a nice experience, I could see why it is held in such high esteem, considered one of the best places to retreat for meditation and Buddhism. It was also particularly famous for a person called Osel Torres, a Spanish boy that had been proclaimed a lama, Lama Tenzin Osel Rinpoche. He had struggled with such a responsibility and eventually retired to the island of Ibiza in his native Spain to live his life normally.

Pleased I had made the effort to come I left the Kopan Monastery with half a thought that I would love to return in future maybe like one of the students I saw on the grass to learn more, who knows?

Next on the list was Gokarna Hindu temple. It was a few kilometres away along a dusty track and through some woods; it was a lovely warm day for a walk.

I was lost in thought as I made my to Gokarna Mahadev, the journey was meant to be less than an hour but as it was very humid and sticky, and Holi meaning every time you passed someone you stopped to wish them 'happy happy Holi', the journey was a little slower. I quite enjoyed seeing the joy on the well-wisher's faces, I can't think of any festival in the UK, including Christmas that brings out such open warmth in people. Plus, it is amazing how kindness and warmth is infectious.

As I walked, I stumbled into a procession of people playing all sorts of instruments, with bikes and mopeds following tooting their horns with children flitting about gaily squirting water and throwing powders. One particularly mischievous boy threatened to douse me in both and then saw my camera and politely wished me 'namaste' before running off.

My lonely planet, printed in December 2015 (it was now March 2016) should not have been out of date, it read that the temple was sat beside the Bagmati river which was supposedly a clear mountain stream. I now considered this was irony, looking back on my first experience of this same river further along in Pashupatinath.

I didn't have to pay an entrance fee for this temple as it was ostensibly closed as all practicing Hindus were outside celebrating Holi, there was no one left to police the entrance fees. Although I could wander about the temples unmolested, I was unable to enter them, which was a shame.

On the face of it the temples had also suffered some damage from the earthquake, though the main three-tiered pagoda still looked pretty good. This temple was dedicated to the great god Shiva (Mahadeva), the embodiment of enlightenment to Hindus. Surrounding the main pagoda were other smaller temples and shrines, one in particular was set into a tree that was particularly interesting. The whole place was quiet and peaceful, so I just sat a while in the idyllic space away from the mania of Holi and Thamel. Although I couldn't go inside, I thoroughly enjoyed Gokarna and its energy. I was able to just be still for a while which was all I was looking for and was equally why I had enjoyed Kopan too.

As the sun dipped on the horizon to the west, lengthening the shadows I decided to make my way back into Kathmandu, one of my last tasks on this trip was souvenir shopping for gifts for the family, my pilgrimage to the Himalayas was drawing to a close.

Day 26 – Kathmandu

23/3/2016

I did my shopping as planned the evening before on my way back from Gokarna after having a coffee. I came across a man on a side street with a huge amount of items, I was surprised he was there as there were literally no people around, maybe he was a kind of 'Del Boy', popping into existence for a short time before melting into the crowd as necessary. In any case he had just what I was looking for from masks of Buddha and Ganesh, as well as mini Ganesh statuettes (Ganesh stands for protection and power and is a safeguard against obstacles) and Gurkha knives. All in all, I spent about a hundred pounds, but I think I managed to get quite a lot for that and was happy with the mementos.

In the morning, I think my body was ready for the end and was now enjoying the relaxation, I struggled to rouse myself much before 9:00am, extremely late comparatively to what I had been doing over the past few weeks. I decided that it might be nice for a wander up to the natural history museum near the monkey temple I had visited before and a good walk across town, giving me an opportunity for one last real look at the city.

With my headphones in I set off and must have been lost in my thoughts as although I had done this walk a few times I suddenly came to and realized I had been walking far too long. It was interesting though as I entered an area I hadn't previously that was peppered with collapsed buildings and people in tents or under tarpaulins, much like near Boudha stupa. Like that area, there were also new large apartment blocks (four or five storeys) sat empty and non-existent roads and ditches had been dug where presumably piping and cables were to be lain. It was as if they were building first and thinking of the logistics afterwards. No real planning and seemingly no workmen.

After asking a few shop keepers I found the museum on the south slopes of the hill of the monkey temple. It was literally one long red bricked building, much like a barracks; I was intrigued as to what would be housed there. I paid my entry fee as well as a surcharge to be able to take photos, of what though I was not sure.

Stepping into the building, the musty smell was quite strong, and the scene was like something from the Victorian age. There were stuffed animals and rows of jars with specimens floating in formaldehyde as well as cases of birds and reptiles screwed onto branches with hand painted foliage. At one point there were even jars containing specimens of baby elephants, disfigured goats and pigs. It was all a bit macabre. On the top of another bookcase stood a rhesus macaque (stuffed) carrying a bag wearing a national hat. In its time clearly one for the children and tourists to laugh at, in this day and age though completely inappropriate, a bit tasteless and more than a little bit creepy.

The electronic exhibit room was out of action due to load shedding, though from what I could gather it was not so much video screens as just lightboxes that lit when you pushed a button to match up animals and habitats. Like the general area there were many signs of the earthquake, this was a stone's throw from the monkey temple that had suffered badly so wasn't really surprising.

I wandered the dusty exhibits for about half an hour and in that time was the only visitor. There was a man and woman wandering about who appeared to be discussing the layout of the exhibits, presumably to improve the flow, they would need a hell of a lot more than just moving things around I thought.

Exiting I made way slowly back to Thamel. This was it; I was feeling a bit blue as the realization that this fabulous trip was now over. I would pack and relax preparing for my flight at 4:00pm the next day.

Day 27 – Kathmandu

24/3/2016

I would end my trip as I started, in the wonderful Garden of Dreams. With a few hours to kill before leaving for the airport, I could think of nothing better and of nowhere better to be. Just to sit and reflect on this most memorable and magical of experiences.

Nepal had always been a draw to me, I had dreamed of coming ever since I was 15 trying to convince my parents to let me come on a teaching program. As a destination it had not disappointed. Sagarmartha was incredible, it was everything I could have hoped for. It had been a spiritual experience as well as a reflective one and had provided the space to clear my head and my heart. Coming in the off season had definitely been the wise choice as my intention to have some quiet walking time, on what is one of the worlds most popular trekking routes would have been unlikely had I departed even a week later. I had seen the start of the season making my way back down from EBC and the sheer number of people coming the other way. I have no doubt that this would have ruined the experience which I had yearned for, a solitary one.

Kathmandu had been surprising in so many ways. Clearly devastated by the earthquake it has so much to offer a visitor, however it desperately needs to get its act together. A small example was the load shedding, I had found it completely unlivable at the start but by the end was just an irritation. The locals seem to acquiesce to the point that it is now seen as an accepted norm, no one talks of when or how it will change; and it is this mentality of acquiescence that I think has permeated every aspect of their lives, so much so that they don't appear to look for change or betterment. It is how it is, and that is how it shall be.

Over all the city, it felt like a place on its knees, half hoping to stand, half happy where it was as long as it didn't completely fall over. The cup half empty half full argument. It was a shame I had been unable to go to the second city of Pokhara to compare.

In the city, pollution is an ever present, from the air you breath as you walk amongst the heavy traffic of diesel trucks and mopeds as there are very few pavements in the old towns, to the sewage laden holy rivers and streams crisscrossing the city emitting their fetid, putrid smells with a haze of flies and mosquitos dancing on their surfaces. As I mentioned earlier, for a country that literally survives off the back of its awesome nature and environment, to be so wantonly ignorant in the city of such simple things as putting rubbish in a bin and not a river, its exasperating to see.

The traffic, a large cause of the pollution, is so chaotic, the lack of road rules (seemingly) or road markings make any journey a genuine free for all. It really is no exaggeration to say you are putting your life in your drivers hands when you hop into a little Suzuki and weave between humongous Chinese or Indian trucks spewing their toxic fumes, even more so when you are walking along the side of the road relying on the drivers being aware. After a day or so you do get used to it, but on arrival it seems utter madness.

All of these issues might seem solvable if the powers that be could get their acts together, but Nepalese politics is clearly an issue, extreme groups failing to agree mean a country divided and unable to move forward. Saying that though, rumours of agreements with India to build two massive hydroelectric dams in the mountains might be the start of a new beginning (and an end to that horrendous load shedding).

This inability to get things done has done little more than encourage corruption, as it is in many nations trying to stabilize in an ever-changing world. Greasing the palm can often be the only guarantee to move things forward rather than face the red tape of bureaucracy, or as in the case of Nepal, the complete lack of it. I had seen money change hands with officials and officers at various times, be it roadside stops or official checkpoints.

Looking up from my notes, it was nice to see on my last visit to the Garden of Dreams that they were renovating, painting the sun faded walls. I saw this as symbolic for the city, on the cusp of rejuvenation, at least I hope this was a sign of the future.

The cost of visiting Nepal is genuinely what you want it to be. As much as one can stay in a high-end boutique hotel eating largely westernized foods drinking typically famous branded alcohol, you can stay in guest houses and eat local foods. Food is generally an expensive item throughout Nepal, especially on the trails, as far as day to day prices go, yet average accommodations are not, so it evens itself out.

I think two types of people choose to come to Nepal, trekkers or hippies looking for spiritual enlightenment, maybe with the aid of some herbal substances. It most definitely is a trekkers paradise and I could only hope I would get the chance to come again, maybe with a loved one to share it with.

Bhutan had not been on the initial agenda when I had planned my pilgrimage to the Everest, but oh wow, when the opportunity arose what a truly magical, spiritual, beautiful place. Although expensive I cannot argue that it has not managed to maintain a fine equilibrium between tourism and sustainability. As an outsider I hope they manage to continue their unique nation and culture, it was really an honour to have experienced such a place.

The juxtaposition between the modern and traditional is so delicate and the issue of Nepali expulsion aside, which is abhorrent, did help them achieve their current state, the leaders of the nation, especially the 3rd King of Bhutan (Jigme Dorji Wangchuck) needs respect for their management and balancing of the needs of their nation in a constantly and rapidly evolving world. There are few places left on Earth so unique and yet accessible, of course that is if you can afford it.

The spiritual side is infectious too, I have left looking to learn more about Buddhism, Hinduism and the concept of the gross national happiness index, they share values that every human being could benefit from, kindness, charity and a desire to be ones best self, for ourselves, our communities and mankind in general; and the concept that the environmental impact of any decision we make is equally important to the economic impact is one that, should we all follow would surely help us all contribute to a better world.

One day it is a dream to go back to Bhutan, that short time I was there will live long and large in my memory, if I am not blessed to be able to return in the future, I know I will always have those four magical days in the Himalayan kingdom to remember.

All in all, the trip had given me just what I had been looking for, a spiritual journey or pilgrimage in the Himalayas to, however you want to phrase it, rebalance my Chi, find inner peace or provide a reawakening. I felt more back to myself than I had done in a long time and I was ready to return to normal life and loved ones. I had missed Glaiza terribly and couldn't wait to share my adventure with her.

End

Swayambhunath Stupa – Monkey Temple

Prayer Flags and view from Swayambhunath

Bishnumati River, Kathmandu – Beloved river of Lord Vishnu

A typical stupa in the city

Sagarmartha Travel Permit and TIMS

Durbar Square

Propped up building in Durbar Square

Earthquake damage in Durbar Square

Lukla airstrip – one of the most dangerous in the world. The picture doesn't do the upward slope justice.

My Tara-Air airplane

Day one, refueling as it was quite warm

Porters carry incredible loads

Ticket Office for Sagarmatha National Park

The entrance Gate to the Park

Bridges across the Dudh Koshi river, you can almost hear the metallic creak

Namche Bazaar and memorial to Tenzing Norgay

Jun and I struggling on the road to Tengboche

Tengboche in the morning

Memorials on the road to Lobuche, only the sound of prayer flags fluttering in the wind could be heard

Gorak Shep, the path the Kala Pattar off to the left

Base Camp – a literal pile of stones

Everest and the range from Kala Pattar

Durbar Square, Patan

A 'real' sadhu

The 'crystal clear' Bagmati river at Pashupatinath

Boudhanath Stupa, in a state of serious repair

Butter lamps at Boudhanath stupa

Everest from the skies, en route to Bhutan

National Museum, overlooking the Paro valley

Roadside archery

The Tigers Nest

Tshewang (right) and Kezang (left)

Thimphu in early spring

Buddha Dordenma, the '8th wonder of the world'

Paro Dzong

Paro Tsechu

Clowns at play, Paro Tsechu

Kopan Monastery

Nepal Natural History 'Museum'

Garden of Dreams

Printed in Great Britain
by Amazon